Their Own Worst Enemies

Their Own Worst Enemies

Women Writers of Women's Fiction

Daphne Watson

Pluto **Press**

LONDON • BOULDER, COLORADO

First published 1995 by
Pluto Press
345 Archway Road
London N6 5AA
and 5500 Central Avenue
Boulder, Colorado 80301, USA

PR
8888
. W6
W38
1995

British Library Cataloguing in Publication Data
A catalogue record for this book is available from the British
Library

ISBN 0 7453 0655 1 hbk

Library of Congress Cataloging in Publication Data
Watson, Daphne, 1940–
        Their own worst enemies: women writers of women's
    fiction / by Daphne Watson.
        p. cm.
        Includes bibliographical references (p.) and index.
        ISBN 0–7453–0655–1 (hb)
        1. English fiction—Women authors—History and criticism.
    2. Women—Great Britain—Books and reading—History—20th
    century.
        3. Women and literature—Great Britain—History—20th
    century.
        4. English fiction—20th century—History and criticism. I. Title.
        PR888.W6W38   1995
        823'.91099287—dc   94–5059
                                                              CIP

98   97   96   95
 4   3   2   1

Designed and produced for Pluto Press by
Chase Production Services, Chipping Norton, OX7 5QR
Typeset by Stanford DTP Services
Printed in Finland by WSOY

Contents

Acknowledgements

My thanks for support and encouragement to students and colleagues at Bournemouth University, especially Angela Campbell, Robert Giddings and Malcolm Povey. Also to Tony Warren for his sympathetic interest, and to Anne Beech, Clive Bloom and Christine Considine for their advice and patience.

Introduction

Poesie therefore is an arte of imitation ... a speaking picture:
with this end, to teach and delight ... The poet doth not only
show the way, but giveth so sweete a prospecte into the way,
as will intice any man to enter into it ... with a tale forsooth
hee commeth unto you, with a tale which holdeth children from
play, and old men from the chimney corner.[1]

My foremost concern is how fairy tales operate ideologically
to indoctrinate children so that they will conform to dominant
social standards which are not necessarily established in their
behalf ... Therefore, it is advisable to uncover paradigmatic
patterns, which may correspond to social configurations, to shed
light on the way ideology works.[2]

Both Sir Philip Sidney, writing in 1580, and Jack Zipes, writing
in 1983, express two undeniable truths: that stories exercise considerable power on their hearers/readers, and that through stories
societies may effectively communicate their dominant ideologies.
We are all suckers for stories; their appeal, especially if they are
of the fairy or magic variety, is probably as old as mankind itself.
Through them we construct our image of the world around us,
its rules and roles, its taboos and rewards. Narratives, whether silent
or verbalised, are the means whereby we make meaning out of
reality, which to borrow Eliot's phrase, is otherwise experienced
as confused, fragmentary and random. So, through stories, those
we are told by others and those we tell ourselves, we learn to create
an acceptable self.

My aim in this book is to consider the particular kinds of story
that encourage women to create what seem to them to be
acceptable selves. I shall argue that, contrary to popular belief, it
is not so much male writers who have described women in terms
of stereotypical behaviour patterns, but some of the most popular
women writers of the twentieth century. I shall also argue that
these stereotypical patterns derive largely from the two most
popular literary traditions of the nineteenth century: the
Gothic/Romantic and the fairytale. The kind of stereotyping I am

1

talking about applies to both characterisation and plot and can be found in both the Gothic/Romantic and fairytale genres. Since the former obviously borrowed heavily from the latter, it seems useful to start by looking at the fairytale as it manifests itself in the nineteenth century. In his book *Fairy tales and the Art of Subversion* (1983) Jack Zipes makes a persuasive case for the transformation of the folktale into the fairytale, the latter with a far more limited set of characters and their possible roles, and a highly moral and absolutely closed ending. He follows Walter J Ong[3] in noting what becomes of oral material when it is written down, especially by men. Folktales reflected all kinds of societal structure, including, particularly in Europe, the matriarchal familial patterns and consequent attribution of power to women in the pre-Christian era which the developing male-centred Christian Church could not allow. We can see how, as a result of the teachings of the church we can see how women's roles became strictly defined and their power limited. Even the mother of God is a marginal figure in the physical church, with her very own chapel to be sure, but one well to the side of the central aisle with its focus on the main altar dedicated to the worship of an all-male Trinity: God the Father, God the Son, and God the Holy Ghost. This last being is the most interesting element of all, representing as it does the arrogation of the one kind of power women are, even now, supposed to have, that of the intuitive, imaginative part of being. Mothers, the church says, are acceptable women, but they have their proper place, and that is to be subject to the father. As for the rest of women, they have two possible roles when young, one when old. When young they can be maidens and therefore acceptable, or sexually active and therefore unacceptable. When old, if not defined as someone's – some man's – mother, they are hags, witches, figures now of fun, once of persecution. The power the folktales attributed to them in naming them wise women has been marginalised, even ridiculed. Further, during their active lives, pre-marriage, women are assigned essentially passive roles. As Zipes shows in his analyses of fairytales featuring girls or boys, men or women, only males are allowed to be active; only Jack can climb the beanstalk and kill the ogre; Snow White and Briar Rose must wait in actual sleep to be awakened to life and love by their persistent princes. Angela Carter, in *The Virago Book of Fairy Tales* (1990) has shown that many tales of active, intrepid, intelligent women do exist. What has become of them? They do not fit the Perrault, Grimm, Andersen pattern. They have not been beautifully illustrated by

Arthur Rackham, nor collected famously by Andrew Lang in coloured books. They are not part of the story were told as we were constructing our story of reality. They are not part of our image of the acceptable permitted roles of women. The Gothic novel, too, I shall argue, limits and confines the possible roles of women; the Gothic novel is guilty of even greater subversion than fairytales themselves.

Although the Gothic novel with its relish of horrific events and minimal depth of characterisation clearly has much in common with the Elizabethan novels of such as Greene and Nashe, which were popular at the time Sidney wrote his *Apologie For Poetrie*, the Gothic novel *per se* appeared as a new phenomenon at the end of the eighteenth century. Whereas we can allow that the fairytale, with all its archetypal narratological devices which so easily become stereotypical, simplified and ultimately simplistic, nonetheless had honourable intentions, the same cannot be claimed for the Gothic novel. Arising as it did at the end of the eighteenth century it came to be identified, wrongly I feel, with the concurrent rise of Romanticism. Romanticism, especially as expressed by both Wordsworth and Coleridge in their prose as well as in their poetry, was essentially concerned with the importance and uniqueness of the individual and, it has to be said, *his* experience and perception of the world, and therefore celebrated evidence of that uniqueness regardless of class and education. The writers of Gothic novels showed no such nobility of concept or practice. The Gothic novel was well described by Fanny Burney in her preface to *Evelina* (1778):

> Romance: where Fiction is coloured by all the gay tints of luxurious Imagination, where Reason is an outcast, and where the sublimity of the Marvellous rejects all aid from sober Probability.[4]

Like her immediate successor Jane Austen, Burney clearly had no time for this truly novel form of fiction. Austen made her feelings clear explicitly and implicitly in *Northanger Abbey* (1818), where her heroine Catherine Morland is so influenced by her reading of one particularly popular practitioner of Gothic fiction, Ann Radcliffe, that she is unable to see the world that is really about her for what it actually is. A man cannot simply be widowed, he must have murdered his wife. His house, so fortuitously and

Gothically named Northanger Abbey with all its concomitant asso-
ciations of bricked-up nuns and ghostly hauntings, gives Catherine
a sleepless night; her imagination so runs riot. And it is Ann
Radcliffe whose narrative structure, types of character and plot
devices most probably influenced subsequent nineteenth- and
twentieth-century writers of this kind of fiction. Ann Radcliffe is
by no means the best, if one can call it that, exponent of what
became recognisably the Gothic tradition. Horace Walpole's
Castle of Otranto (1764), with its extraordinary events so flatly told
that the whole project must have been as much a joke as his house
at Strawberry Hill, is probably the funniest as well as the first Gothic
novel. William Beckford's *Vathek* (1782) is written in a similarly
arch manner, such that the excesses described become, as they
do to Vathek himself, too much of a good thing:

> But what a sight for a father's eyes! He beheld his child dashed
> to pieces, and almost buried under an enormous helmet, an
> hundred times more large than any casque ever made for
> human being, and shaded with a proportionable quantity of
> black feathers.[5]

This, from the very first page of *Otranto* with its so judicious use
of the word 'proportionable', surely gives the game away? The writer
rejects that most desirable of narrative devices, suspense, and
plunges us *in medias res* without any preparation whatsoever.
Beckford, likewise in *Vathek*, by means of an apparently casual
opening description of his hero, reveals his ironic detachment from
his creation:

> His figure was pleasing and majestic; but when he was angry,
> one of his eyes became so terrible, that no person could bear
> to behold it; and the wretch upon whom it was fixed instantly
> fell backward, and sometimes expired. For fear, however, of
> depopulating his dominions and making his palace desolate,
> he but rarely gave way to his anger.[6]

No such irony leavens Ann Radcliffe's interminable narrative in
The Mysteries of Udolpho (1794). She wholeheartedly believes in
the wickedness of her villain, Montoni. In her delineation of
him, his appearance, sinister past and exotic setting she creates
a narratological paradigm which must be familiar to any reader
of *Jane Eyre* or *Rebecca*, not to mention all the novels of Mary Stewart
and the whole 'modern Gothic' movement (as it is termed by

Joanna Russ in her essay 'Somebody's Trying to Kill Me and I Think it's My Husband: The Modern Gothic' (1973), as well as the Mills & Boon novel. Montoni's looks (tall and dark and strangely powerful), as well as his behaviour (the murder of a wife, the abduction and almost-seduction of a chaste heroine), not to mention his habitation (remote mountain fastnesses in strange and foreign lands – France and Italy actually) recur in subsequent fiction as almost obligatory elements of the romantic hero. Radcliffe's mode of narration, too, the events succeeding one another breathlessly, one perilous situation avoided only for the heroine, Emily, to fall foul of yet another of Montoni's wicked plots, reminds one of the endless sequence of incidents that constitute plot for writers like Jackie Collins and Shirley Conran.

Jane Austen was right to criticise Radcliffe specifically because of the disservice she does to women. Unlike Austen's own lively and flawed heroines, Emily is goodness and virtue personified, but otherwise she is nothing, a cipher representing opposition to Montoni. Faced with crisis she swoons, awakening to find the villain has fortunately decided not to take advantage of her. She plays her lute, and practises her many accomplishments as an eighteenth-century young lady should. She never confronts Montoni, never even tries to escape from his clutches; like Briar Rose she waits for her equally cipher-like hero, Valancourt, to save her.

The Gothic novel, then, can be seen to have little in common with Romanticism; it is concerned with sensationalism rather than sensibility, and has borrowed from the fairytale in a simplistic manner. It is concerned with a world that is black or white; it is not concerned with individuation; unlike the Romantic movement it does not present us with the *bildungsroman*. Emily learns nothing from her experiences, unlike Jane Austen's heroines or those of Charlotte and Emily Brontë.

In the Gothic novel, as in the fairytale as related by Perrault, Andersen and the brothers Grimm, we find a pervasive set of male/female characteristics, of both appearance and role play. The heroine is essentially passive, always beautiful, awaiting either in sleep or in a prison which denies her ability to act, her awakening or enfranchisement by the active if not always necessarily handsome hero. She is threatened in her virtue by wicked but often mysteriously attractive villains. She is also often under threat from villainous hags. For, as I said earlier, the roles for older women are limited, and if by any chance they are unpleasing to look at, never mind deformed, they must be wicked – witches in fact. *Active* women are almost always up to no good (an interesting point *vis-à-vis* Dale Spender's theories concerning gender-charged language[7] is that here as elsewhere the female version of a positive male role, the wizard, is totally negative).

It is my contention that in our society no less than in that of the nineteenth century women are bombarded with negative images and a reinforcement of a narrowly patriarchal societal structure which is scarcely palliated by the roles allotted to women in soaps and other television series, not to mention advertising. Where, then, might one find positive images? In feminist fiction certainly; in the novels of writers like Margaret Atwood and Angela Carter; and in science fantasy where the freedom to create new worlds and new societal structures allows writers like Sally Miller Gearhart, Mary Gentle, Marge Piercy to offer very different images of possible roles for women. But what of popular women's fiction? And by popular I mean the kind of fiction read by every kind of woman. Science fantasy has its fans and feminist fiction a wide readership among students, academics, *Guardian* readers and watchers of the *Late Show*, but none of these writers can claim the automatic bestseller status of a Jackie Collins, the automatic reprinting of a Mary Stewart or a Dorothy L Sayers, the subscription network of Mills & Boon. This kind of popular fiction, I shall argue, relies essentially for its narratological structure, its male/female characterisation, on the paradigmatic structure of the fairytale. Whether the outcome be positive or negative, in the sense of 'happy-ever-after' or, as in the case of Brookner's and Pym's heroines, 'unhappy-ever-after', the essential basic premise is that of the passive princess awaiting her awakening by the active prince. This paradigm informs even that genre apparently more concerned with the 'reality' of criminality and violence, the detective story. From Dorothy L Sayers' Lord Peter Wimsey to P D James's Adam Dalgliesh, through Margery Allingham's aristo in disguise, Albert Campion, and the overtly aristocratic Roderick Alleyn of Ngaio Marsh or Inspector Grant of Josephine Tey, one cannot help but feel that Poe's and Conan Doyle's genre has been changed; where once the reader found reason she now finds emotion; logical deduction has given way to romantic fiction. And it is in these novels, as well as those of Daphne du Maurier and Mary Stewart, where the influence is perhaps more obvious, that we can detect that other influential nineteenth-century literary strand, the Gothic novel.

That such a development was not inevitable, and that there was an alternative tradition is, I think, important to emphasise, especially given the ways in which Charlotte Brontë's *Jane Eyre* has been 'borrowed' by many of the writers I shall be discussing in this book. This alternative literary tradition offered the nineteenth-century woman reader a different reading of her possible role in life – her potential for and right to personal fulfilment. Following in the tradition of Jane Austen and her detailed scrutiny of the actual society of her day and her heroines' struggle for self-knowledge, George Eliot and Elizabeth Gaskell continue to develop the novel as image of real world. But the Brontës, especially Charlotte, could be said to have done more; they attempted to marry that tradition with the perception of the extraordinary within the ordinary that could be seen to be the best legacy of the Romantic movement. Despite feminist criticisms of Charlotte Brontë's presentation of an active sexual woman as the 'madwoman in the attic',[8] Bertha Mason, and despite her having apparently fallen into the patriarchal trap of condemning women for practising what men take for granted as their sole right – witness Rochester's almost boastful 'confession' of his past conquests – much more significant for the time she was writing is Brontë's creation of heroines who are emphatically not beautiful and who are active in the pursuit of their own independence and fulfilment. Jane's thoughts as she walks the leads at Thornfield Hall, having found a pleasant place to live and work, among congenial people, must have come as a shock to the Victorian reader:

> I longed for a power of vision which might ... reach the busy world, towns, regions full of life I had heard of but never seen; that then I desired more of practical experience than I possessed; more of intercourse with my kind, of acquaintance with variety of character, than was here within my reach ...
>   It is vain to say that human beings ought to be satisfied with tranquillity: they must have action; ... Millions are condemned to a stiller doom than mine, and millions are in silent revolt against their lot. Nobody knows how many rebellions besides political rebellions ferment in the masses of life which people earth. Women are supposed to be very calm generally: but women feel just as men feel; they need exercise for their faculties, and a field for their efforts as much as their brothers do; they suffer from too rigid a restraint, too absolute a stagnation, precisely as men would suffer; and it is narrow-

minded in their more privileged fellow-creatures to say that they ought to confine themselves to making puddings and knitting stockings, to playing on the piano and embroidering bags. It is thoughtless to condemn them, or laugh at them, if they seek to do more or learn more than custom has pronounced necessary for their sex.[9]

In her creation and presentation of the characters of Jane Eyre and Lucy Snowe in *Villette*, Charlotte Brontë achieved a concept of the heroine which is very different from all those passive golden-haired nonentities who fulfil men's dreams in the novels of the Gothic era, and who continued to litter the pages of those of Charles Dickens in the nineteenth century. And in their creation of heroes like Heathcliff and Rochester both Charlotte and Emily Brontë escaped from the convention that the hero should be unexceptionably noble and virtuous. In fact it might be argued that they have combined in their heroes, to great effect, the expected actions of the Gothic hero with the nature and mystery of the Gothic villain. The Romantic hero, with all his Byronic connotations, thus moves from the rarefied atmosphere of poetry to the more concrete world of nineteenth-century England. But it is important to note what the Brontës have not done; they have not pretended that their stories take place in another world than that which is the world of all of us.[10] And they have not condemned their heroines to be merely passive admirers. Jane Eyre and Catherine Earnshaw are given as much scope to act, to make mistakes and to suffer as any hero. The Brontës thus challenged that patriarchal image of world and gender roles created by Perrault, reinforced by those other male tellers of Fairytales, Andersen and the brothers Grimm, which also informs the narratives of the Gothic movement, even, especially, those written by a woman, Ann Radcliffe.

However, the 'modern Gothic' which has borrowed so heavily from Brontë, has, like advertising with fairytales, taken only the surface and none of the substance. How often are we told, be it by the anonymous heroine of *Rebecca* or the Stewart governess in *Nine Coaches Waiting*, or *all* Mills & Boon heroines, how despite *their* view of themselves as unattractive they are in fact immediately desired by both heroes and villains because of their charms? Even Anita Brookner's Edith Hope in *Hotel Du Lac* is discovered by her admirer Philip to be an attractive woman when, in one of the most clichéd events in cinema texts, she lets her hair down and removes her old-maidish cardigan. As for the heroes, they are never allowed to be as plain and forceful as a Rochester or a Heathcliff; they are all, from Maxim de Winter on, matinée idols, tall, dark and handsome. Even detective heroes do not escape this obligation: Lord Peter Wimsey and Adam Dalgliesh have sensitive hands and faces to match their sensitive minds, and are both attractive to any woman they meet. Stereotypes abound, reinforcing, never challenging, converting what was, in the Brontës' hands, invention, into convention.

John Cawelti, in his essay, 'The Concept of Formula in the Study of Popular Literature' (1987), has usefully explicated this point:

all cultural products contain a mixture of two kinds of elements: conventions and inventions. Conventions are elements which are known to both the creator and his audience beforehand – they consist of things like favorite plots, stereotyped characters, accepted ideas, commonly known metaphors and other linguistic devices, etc. Inventions, on the other hand, are elements which are uniquely imagined by the creator such as new kinds of characters, ideas, or linguistic forms ...

Convention and invention have quite different cultural functions. Conventions represent familiar shared values; inventions confront us with a new perception or meaning which we have not realized before.[11]

Certainly, given this definition, the novels I shall be discussing can be described as 'conventional'. They all offer one particular pleasure that readers undoubtedly seek, that of a familiar world, peopled by expected characters, participating in a comfortingly predictable story, which is told in a straightforward narrative manner.

And this brings me to the problematic issue I hope to address in this book, that of critically evaluating what are seen to be 'popular' texts. For all the texts I am going to discuss are popular, in the sense that they sell well, are continually being reprinted – as in the case of du Maurier and Sayers – and are made into television series – as in the case of James and Collins. Brookner's Booker prizewinner *Hotel Du Lac* was made into a successful television film; Barbara Pym's stories have been adapted for radio and are to be serialised on television. You can see them everywhere, in airports and railway stations, on carousels in supermarkets. They are undoubtedly bestsellers. Like soaps, with which in terms of offering the pleasures of the known they have much in common, they have largely escaped being discussed as *literary* works *per se* (rather as if their very popularity put them off-limits as a topic for critical analysis) and, where they have been discussed, by Janice Radway, Tania Modleski, Joanna Russ, David Margolies, Resa Dudowitz for example, they have been approached with some care. The implication of their popularity suggests somehow that they are part of the mass media and ought therefore to be treated with the kind of respect that media theorists like Stuart Hall have given to texts like *Coronation Street*.

'Popularity' in this context implies that consideration of the readership and its reasons for reading must be taken into account even more than when we are applying reader-response theory to acknowledged literary texts, such as those to which Wolfgang Iser himself applied his reader-oriented criticism. Thus if we take Scholes' and Kellogg's narrative theory model:

Real   Implied   Implied Real
author — author — Narrator — Narratee — reader — reader[12]

we see that it posits the writer–reader relationship in such a way as to position the actual addressee at some distance, implied *critical* distance from the text. If we analyse the structure of *Jane Eyre* according to this model, one which is generally accepted by all writers on narrative theory, we find the following.

1. The real writer is Charlotte Brontë.
2. The implied author is the kind of person who might have written such a text, with all its moral burden.
3. The narrator is the character Jane Eyre, telling her story as a mature adult in first person retrospective narration.
4. The narratee is the 'reader' whom she directly addresses.
5. The implied reader is the reader for whom we suppose Brontë wrote the text; in other words a construct of her imagination, at any rate a person of her own time, and carrying all the psycho-social baggage of that time.
6. The real reader is any actual person reading the text.

But for Radway and Modleski in particular, discussion of both the implied and the real reader takes precedence over discussion of actual texts. Radway and Modleski seem to feel it incumbent upon them to deny that the two might be in any way similar. Thus although the implied reader of a Mills & Boon romance might be predicated as a woman, of any age, seeking an escape from her dull, perhaps domestic existence into a fantasy world, Radway and Modleski both emphasise the concept of an interactive reader who is quite unlike the passive consumer (implied reader) suggested by the predictable conventions of the format. I take fuller issue with these critics in the chapter on Mills & Boon novels (Chapter 4); suffice it to say that I am by no means persuaded by their arguments. At no point do any theorists concerned with reader-response deny that readers bring to the text all the psycho-social baggage of their historical situation. Indeed that, as I understand it, is basic to their various expositions of their theories. My argument is concerned with the nature of the baggage that women carry with them as readers real or implied.

My argument, begun in this Introduction and continued throughout the book, is that too many of the texts women encounter, from babyhood onward, offer only a partial, a patriarchal, interpretation of reality. Thus are gender roles reinforced and alternative modes of being rarely if ever held up to scrutiny. It is illuminating, in this context, to see how the various film and television versions of du Maurier's *Rebecca* have failed to offer anything other than an extremely simplistic reading of the problematic natures of Maxim and the two Mrs de Winters. The same has of course too often been true of adaptations of *Jane Eyre* and *Wuthering Heights*. What in fact has happened, and this bears out my contention that the influence of the Gothic has been at best to simplify, at worst to debase a more complex literary tradition, is that these texts, which sought to challenge conventional views of how heroes and heroines should look and behave, have been adapted to fit into the conventions of the romance. The last television adaptation of *Jane Eyre,* for example, starred (note term) Timothy Dalton as Rochester. However good an actor Dalton may be, he could not act the plain and unhandsome man Brontë gives us in her text.

Supporting her belief in the interactive nature of women readers' relationship with 'romance' texts, Janice Radway says:

> For example, no matter how simple popular novels appear on the surface, they are always composed of a linear narrative whose temporal stages and ultimate meaning must be actively constructed by individuals from material encountered only sequentially and in piecemeal form.[13]

This tenet is of course at the heart of reader-response theory, but Iser was referring to the act of reading such challenging texts as *Tristram Shandy* and *Finnegan's Wake*. Obviously the reader here is forced to construct meaning, as she encounters the text. But is this challenge encountered in the reading of the kinds of popular fiction I shall be discussing in this book? I think not, and this is a further issue I shall be addressing. As readers we are forced to become aware of the reading process only if the writer draws our attention to it, by foregrounding the text as a construct, for example, as Margaret Atwood does in *Cat's Eye* (1988). Like the fairytales we listened to in childhood, popular novels are popular because they make no such demands upon us; we do not have to jump from point of view to point of view as we do with Tilly Olsen's *Yonnondio* (1973), or *Tell Me a Riddle* (1962); we do not have to construct meaning out of lies, deception and half-truths, as we do with Atwood's *Surfacing* (1972). The appeal of the popular novel is that it draws us instantly into its world, provides us with a stable narrative voice, and tells us its story in a straightforward manner. It may often employ suspense, surprising revelations, but in the end it fulfils our childhood expectations of a story: it provides escape into a fantasy world where the writer is in control, and where satisfying closure is always provided. Essentially, therefore it *acts* on the reader in the way in which a fairytale does; by means of its familiar structure, in terms of plot, characterisation and seductive narrative flow, it actually recalls to the reader all her psycho-social baggage. It reinforces because it fulfils expected narratological patterns. We do not look in this kind of fiction for experimentation of the kind Cawelti meant when he wrote of 'invention'.[14] So what do we find, whether in terms of style, narrative structure or characterisation, when we analyse popular fiction written by women for women? In his entertaining and perceptive book, *Language in Popular Fiction* (1990), Walter Nash outlines the ways in which women's fiction, or 'popfiction' as he calls it, is written:

> This ideological view of domestic woman, obedient and triumphant, governs the broad patterning of the stories and ultimately controls the detail of recurrent stylistic devices. In constructing their narratives, the authors habitually make use of three interlinked elements. One of these is *Relation*, that is, the description of the characters, their actions, and the events in which they are progressively involved; a second is *Dialogue*; and the third, for which it is necessary to invent a special term,

is *Dilation*. The word 'dilation' punningly connects 'relation' and 'dialogue' ... What is principally meant by Dilation, however, is a widening of the field of narrative unaccompanied by an onward movement of the plot – as when the author or the narrator-within-the-tale 'dilates' on matters complementary to the story.[15]

Nash very usefully points out how this differentiates women's from men's or 'adventure' fiction. Men are concerned with the onward movement of the plot, and very rarely with what the characters think, especially about themselves. Women's fiction on the contrary is continually self-reflexive; women 'feel', anxiety usually, about their looks, the way the hero is seeing them, what he will say; even worse, they continually analyse what might have happened had they done or said something. What women's fiction also does, and this essentially is the argument of this book, is to confirm the reader in her view of herself as society would like her to be; in the end all that matters is the love of a good man, and acceptance of the way she looks, dresses, decorates her house, *behaves*, by that all-important patriarchal structure we call society.

In order to explicate and justify my position I have deliberately chosen a wide variety of texts, not just those which most obviously fall into the category women's fiction, such as the novels of Mills & Boon, Jackie Collins and Shirley Conran. It is my contention that writers who appear to have chosen to write according to the demands of other genres, notably the detective story or the comedy of manners, tend very often even while writing undeniably 'good reads' to fall into the stereotypical narratological trap of using stereotypical male/female characters along with an expected, indeed familiar story structure. Their heroines may not always end by living happily ever after with their princes, but that that is their aim and desire is both clear and a negation of any possible alternative reading of what kind of life a woman might have. I have also chosen writers whose implied readers may be different. Although of course real readers read anything and everything. However, there is no doubt that certain of the writers I have chosen assume that their readers are pretty well educated. Mary Stewart, for example, loads her novels with a freight of literary reference, echo and allusion, which implies a literary sophistication similar to that expected of Dorothy L Sayers' readers who must be *au fait* with metaphysical poetry and French in order to enter into the world of her extremely well-educated and highly intelligent hero and heroine. Barbara Pym and Anita Brookner also make no allowances for an unread readership. So many of their heroines are involved in the world of academe, libraries, literature, that the reader too is supposed to be alive to quotations, acknowledged or not, and to appreciate the irony of a heroine engaged upon a book on Balzac while patently failing to learn from his observations on how the world goes. It would be easy to mistake this vaunted erudition for superior perception; to mistake an elegantly turned phrase for evidence of an attitude of mind far removed from the simple-sentence lovers of the Mills & Boon preferred mode of expression, or the Capitalised sentences beloved of Jackie Collins.

My argument is not with style, or at least only in passing. What I am concerned with is the appearance and reappearance of the familiar narratological patterns of plot and characterisation: passive fairytale princesses rescued by active handsome princes, the implication that love is the only thing that matters, that women must eternally define themselves in terms of patriarchal expectations. Therefore I have chosen a variety of writers who might be expected to appeal to a variety of readers. My interest is also in seeing whether, and if so how far the different demands of genre in fact produce difference. Or whether in fact these writers superficially very different from one another actually utilise those twin literary heritages, the fairytale and the Gothic novel in a very similar manner.

The writers I have chosen are essentially representative both of the popular novel and of the various subgenres to which they belong. I begin with a chapter on the novels of Daphne du Maurier and Mary Stewart as they seem to me to represent elements derived from the nineteenth-century fairytale/Gothic traditions, as well as providing a useful basis for the investigation of certain recurrent patterns of setting, theme, plot and characterisation which manifest themselves in the work of other of the writers to be discussed. I have followed this with two chapters on writers who at first sight may appear to be of rather different kinds, Barbara Pym and Anita Brookner in Chapter 2, and Dorothy L Sayers and P D James in Chapter 3. I was interested to discover whether these writers did indeed render women differently, since, as I have suggested earlier, their perceived readership might well be different, given the literariness of the first two and the genre obligations of the latter two. In Chapters 4 and 5 I have looked at two again apparently differing phenomena, the Mills & Boon novel and the so-called 'blockbuster', certainly best-selling novels of three writers typical of this genre: Jackie Collins, Shirley Conran and Sally Beauman. These latter novels have not been the subject of much literary criticism to date, and the work done by Radway and Modleski, though thorough, is in fact concerned with the American version of the Mills & Boon novel, the Harlequin. Mills & Boon novels and 'blockbuster' or 'sex and shopping' novels as those of Conran et al have been described, are immensely popular. What I am concerned with is an attempt to analyse the ingredients that have rendered them so, and to place them, together with those other novels whose perceived aims might well be of a nobler order, in terms of their contribution to women's perception of the world in which they live.

In the Conclusion I discuss the relevance of these novels to today's women; the problems created by the existence of a quite different male 'script', from which we may suppose men learn their expected roles; and where the popular novel for women, by women, might go. Where it more clearly is going, given the challenge of Joanna Russ or the charms of Joanna Trollope, is, I fear, all too obvious.

1

Reader, I Married Him:
The Novels of Daphne du Maurier
and Mary Stewart

... after roughly ten years of devotion to the form, romance readers no longer found the experience prompted by the modern gothic enjoyable, useful, or necessary.[1]

In her 1981 essay 'The Utopian Impulse in Popular Literature: Gothic Romances and "Feminist Protest"', Janice Radway suggested that women readers now preferred the attractions offered by detective fiction and by the 'sex and shopping' blockbusters of Collins, Conran, et al. But any glance at the carousels in airports and supermarkets today will prove Radway mistaken. The modern Gothic is alive and well, in reprint form if nothing else. The novels of Daphne du Maurier and Mary Stewart have just been reprinted yet again. Stewart's latest titles (*Thornyhold* (1988) and *Stormy Petrel* (1991)) immediately became bestsellers, and there is no doubt that these novels, old-fashioned though Radway may think them, represent a direct link with those twin literary traditions outlined and discussed in the Introduction: the fairytale and the Gothic novel. These two authors also embody the possibilities and the limitations of the genre of the modern Gothic. Whereas du Maurier, as an exploratory and innovative novelist, raises more questions than she answers, and, despite their Gothic/Romantic trappings, gives her characters the problematic complexities of real people, Stewart is the mistress of closure. Her stories are rattling good yarns, but despite their heavy burden of literary reference rely on simplistic plots and characterisation which reinforce concepts of gender roles more akin to Mrs Radcliffe than Brontë. She seems, despite her efforts to appear up to date, to be trapped forever in that kind of literature which can most kindly be described as escapist. She, and this is the point of my discussion of her here, is one of the true foremothers of the formula novel. I will consider her work later in this chapter.

To set Stewart's work in context, and to offer a yardstick by which she can be fairly judged, let us first consider the novels of Daphne du Maurier, a writer whose work derives from Brontë rather than Radcliffe. Consider these two quotations:

> I looked with timorous joy towards a stately house; I saw a blackened ruin.[2]

> Last night I dreamt I went to Manderley again ... No smoke came from the chimney, and the little lattice windows gaped forlorn.[3]

This latter quotation, perhaps one of the most famous openings to a novel, reveals from the outset and in an obvious way the debt du Maurier owed to Brontë, one she was very ready to acknowledge. However it is my contention that the undoubted success of *Rebecca* (1938), as a novel, a film and a TV serial, and the lesser but no less interesting successes of other du Maurier novels such as *Jamaica Inn* (1936), *Frenchman's Creek* (1941), *The King's General* (1946), and *My Cousin Rachel* (1951), owe much to the way in which *several* nineteenth-century fictive themes and devices resonate in them, not least the Brontës' brilliance at melding the ordinary and the fantastic in order to expand the reader's imagination and perception of the real world. Of course, *Jane Eyre* can be seen, depending on your interpretation of Charlotte Brontë, as a supporter or traitor to the feminist cause. The latter view would see the novel as a very moral tale about the proper relationship between man and woman, even a cautionary tale, in the Victorian manner, for any woman who believes she has the right to the same kind of sexual fulfilment permitted to a man. However there is the other point of view, that *Jane Eyre* represents a feminist version of the experience of love as a transcendent experience reserved by writers of the Romantic period for men only. Jane's love for Rochester transcends narrow morality; she leaves him because morality (or conscience) tells her to. But never for an instant does she forget him. His despairing call to her, like their love itself, transcends the parameters of space; their marriage is a fusion of two into one and blissful, not just conventionally happy ever after. *Jane Eyre* was thus a daring assault upon the perceived parameters of female experience and behaviour. Daphne du Maurier, I shall argue, follows in *this* aspect of the Brontë/Romantic tradition.

Superficially it would appear that du Maurier has, in effect, rewritten Jane Eyre's story in so far as it is also Cinderella's story. Here, in *Rebecca*, we find a child-bride, a first-person narrator so self-denying she doesn't even have a name other than Mrs de Winter. Here is Maxim, the handsome older hero, with a magnificent family seat, a fortune, a gathering of retainers, and an actual skeleton, in his bay rather than in his cupboard. Here is the mysterious house, haunted by reminders of his first, dead love. And here too is the condemnatory revelation of the true and wicked nature of that first dead wife:

> You thought I loved Rebecca? ... You thought I killed her, loving her? I hated her, I tell you. Our marriage was a farce from the very first. She was vicious, damnable, rotten through and through. We never loved each other, never had one moment of happiness together. Rebecca was incapable of love, of tenderness, of decency. She was not even normal.[4]

Even allowing for a little natural exaggeration, given the circumstances, this all sounds suspiciously over the top. Surely he once loved Rebecca, or did he marry her only for the cachet her beauty and charm would bring to Manderley? I shall return to Maxim's own darker nature in a moment; first let us consider the most significant crime adduced against Rebecca. 'She was not even normal.' This word 'normal' is horribly reminiscent of Rochester's tirade in *Jane Eyre* about his wife Bertha:

> I lived with that woman upstairs four years, and before that time she had tried me indeed: her character ripened and developed with frightful rapidity; her vices sprang up fast and rank: they were so strong, only cruelty could check them, and I would not use cruelty. What a pigmy intellect she had, and what giant propensities! How fearful were the curses those propensities entailed on me! Bertha Mason, the true daughter of an infamous mother, dragged me through all the hideous and degrading agonies which must attend a man bound to a wife at once intemperate and unchaste.[5]

Note that this 'intemperance' and 'unchastity' *precede* her madness; as for Maxim with Rebecca, so it is Bertha's expression of her sexuality which leads Rochester to reject her. Implicit in the outbursts of both men is the acknowledgement that the *second* woman is different. Rochester has already made the comparison explicitly before his would-be wedding guests:

That is *my wife* ... such is the sole conjugal embrace I am ever
to know – such are the endearments which are to solace my
leisure hours ! And *this* is what I wished to have ... this young
girl, who stands so grave and quiet at the mouth of hell, looking
collectedly at the gambols of a demon. I wanted her just as a
change after that fierce ragôut. Wood and Briggs, look at the
difference! Compare these clear eyes with the red balls yonder
– this face with that mask – this form with that bulk; then judge
me, priest of the gospel and man of the law.[6]

Du Maurier allows for an implicit comparison, showing how
differently the second Mrs de Winter is perceived by all of Maxim's
friends and relations. They are surprised by her youth, her unworld-
liness, her lack of interest in clothes and hairstyles. All this surprise
underlines Maxim's own interest in her; she is child-like, malleable;
he can impress his own vision of the world upon her:

I ask you [to marry him] ... because you are not dressed in black
satin, with a string of pearls, nor are you thirty-six ... It's a pity
you have to grow up.[7]

But grow up she does, and Maxim laments it in an interesting and
significant passage:

I only mind for you ... I don't regret anything else. If it had to
come all over again I should not do anything different. I'm glad
I killed Rebecca. I shall never have any remorse for that, never,
never. But you. I can't forget what it has done to you ... It's
gone forever, that funny, young, lost look that I loved. It won't
come back again. I killed that too, when I told you about
Rebecca ... It's gone, in twenty-four hours. You are so much
older ...[8]

This is a pivotal moment in the novel; Maxim has at last become
aware of a change in his wife. Since she now knows Rebecca was
'evil and vicious and rotten',[9] she has become the true mistress
of the house, not the *second*, but *the* Mrs de Winter; her emergence
in this role is manifested in her treatment of the servants; now,
she is arrogant not only towards Mrs Danvers, who has deserved
it, but also towards Maud, the under-housemaid, who hasn't.[10]

In her interesting essay on *Rebecca*,[11] Alison Light makes the
point that Rebecca represents a threat to the bourgeois middle-

class view of woman. As Mrs Danvers reveals to a shocked audience (of three men and one woman), men were a 'game' to Rebecca:

> She was not in love with you, or with Mr de Winter. She was not in love with anyone. She despised all men. She was above all that ...
>   Love-making was a game with her, only a game. She told me so. She did it because it made her laugh. It made her laugh, I tell you. She laughed at you like she did at the rest. I've known her come back and sit upstairs in her bed and rock with laughter at the lot of you.[12]

This, not her adultery, was Rebecca's real crime; this is what made her seem evil and vicious: she did not take men seriously. Note that Maxim shoots her while she is laughing at him. Light makes the point, correctly, that although the story is apparently told from a woman's point of view, it is in fact an androcentric or male-oriented point of view. The heroine/narrator reinforces and confirms a *male* view of nonconforming women like Rebecca. The purpose of the 'story' of Rebecca, as opposed to the 'text' of *Rebecca* (to use Genette's terminology) is to reinscribe bourgeois notions of correctness in female behaviour.[13] Light goes on to say that the story helps the second Mrs de Winter to resolve her own problematic sexuality and, by extension, according to Light, that of the female reader. Rebecca transgresses societal codes and is punished for it, not only, as it transpires, by Maxim's shots, but also by fate or even by God – by being endowed with a malformed uterus and suffering from cancer. It is Light's hypothesis that the pleasure women get from reading *Rebecca* is itself androcentric, or manlike, that of finding Rebecca desirable *and* of condemning her.[14] However, while agreeing in part with this reading of the novel and certainly with the perception that, like *Jane Eyre*, *Rebecca* is a novel about class as much as sex, I would argue that the actual 'text' enables du Maurier to permit Rebecca a kind of ultimate victory not granted to poor unfortunate Bertha, who has quite receded from memory by the end of Brontë's novel.

To prove this hypothesis it is necessary, first, to return to the nature of that apparently archetypal hero/villain Maxim de Winter. It is my contention that, the murder of his first wife apart (and I am aware that that is a large caveat), Maxim de Winter is a sheep in wolf's clothing. Certainly, as Light points out, his behaviour is reprehensible; he kills his first wife and disposes of her body in such a way that the term cold-blooded seems too mild a description. Then, within six months he is remarried, this time to a naive innocent young enough to be his daughter. He returns with her to his stately home and appears to take up the threads of his life *as if nothing had happened.* (This is an interesting point to which I shall return.) When the corpse is discovered he makes his second wife an accessory after the fact by confessing to her and persuading her, with the same persuasive techniques as those employed by Rochester – extreme denigration of first wife's sexual propensities allied to over-statement of his own innocent unworld-liness – that he is to be pitied rather than condemned for his crime. He succeeds to such an extent that their roles are ultimately reversed and she, in her retrospective narrative, reveals that she has become mother to his child-like dependence. There is no sense that post-Manderley the de Winter marriage ever attains that idealistic equality expressed in Brontë's novel:

> I know what it is to live entirely for and with what I love best on earth. I hold myself supremely blest – blest beyond what language can express; because I am my husband's life as fully as he is mine. No woman was ever nearer to her mate than I am: ever more absolutely bone of his bone and flesh of his flesh.[15]

It is in this respect that du Maurier has departed from the Brontë pattern; there is no transcendence and blissful union in the love and marriage of the de Winters. Maxim, unlike Rochester, would not appear to have fallen in love with the heroine; rather, as Mrs Hopper, the heroine's unbearable and snobbish American employer, unkindly points out, he is lonely and needs a mistress for his house rather than himself. Of course du Maurier makes us see Mrs Hopper's words as motivated by malice. But if we look at what happens to that heroine after the honeymoon in Venice, which is summarily described, we see behaviour which reinforces Mrs Hopper's point. Maxim brings her straight back to Manderley, no pause for a trousseau – even Rochester managed that – thus exposing her to the scorn of the servants. He then resumes his life, running his estate, popping up to London to his club, leaving his child-bride to find endless reminders of the dead Rebecca. In addition he demands that she make the visits expected of the family by custom. Apart from one ill-fated walk through the Happy Valley together, the couple spend their lives in the company of relatives, the estate manager, the local gentry and the servants. This appears to be what Maxim wants. Only *after* his enforced revelations about his marriage to Rebecca and her subsequent murder does his second marriage appear to be properly consummated:

> He ran his fingers through my hair. Different from his old abstracted way ... Some times he said things to me ... I wondered how it was I could be so happy ... It was a strange sort of happiness. Not what I had dreamt about or expected. It was not the sort of happiness I had imagined in the lonely hours ...[16]

As the heroine says, now she is a child no more. Maxim regrets this at first but soon settles for the new wife – and why not? As she tells us:

> I was free now to be with Maxim, to touch him, and hold him, and love him. I would never be a child again. It would not be I, I, I any longer; it would be we, it would be us. We would be together. We would face this trouble together, he and I. Captain Searle, and the diver, and Frank, and Mrs Danvers, and Beatrice, and the men and women of Kerrith reading their newspapers could not break us now. Our happiness had not come too late. I was not young any more. I was not shy. I was not afraid. I would fight for Maxim. I would lie and perjure and swear, I would blaspheme and pray. Rebecca had not won. Rebecca had lost.[17]

Whether Rebecca has indeed lost is debatable; what is certain is that Maxim has gained, by his confession, an invaluable ally, a far better wife than he could ever have imagined, who will not only do all of the above but will accompany him into exile and comfort his old age, a wife worth more than rubies – but more than Manderley? Maxim admits that he married Rebecca to give Manderley the style it lacked; he put up with her affairs for the sake of Manderley; he killed her because she threatened to make its heir a bastard; he married again to give Manderley a mistress. And in the end he loses Manderley. Whether Mrs Danvers or Jack Favell or accident fired Manderley, Maxim loses it and goes into exile, forfeiting home, position (which clearly matters to him), and country.

Light's perceptive essay notes the appeal of the Rebecca persona but does not in my opinion go far enough. If we consider Rebecca in relation to other popular du Maurier novels an interesting pattern recurs, which would seem to suggest that du Maurier herself is actually on Rebecca's side. And this indicates that she is a very different kind of writer from Mary Stewart. Du Maurier is a writer who is manipulating the fairytale and the Gothic *for her own ends*, to question women's perceived roles and accepted patriarchal structures. Maxim's description of Rebecca, slim and dressed like a boy, is suggestive of du Maurier herself, and the strange relationships with men are redolent of du Maurier's relationships with her father, cousins, and others, as documented in both Judith Cook's *Daphne: A Portrait of Daphne du Maurier* (1991) and, in much clearer and more explicit detail, Margaret Forster's *Daphne du Maurier*, (1993). Du Maurier wrote, just before her husband's death: 'There is no such thing as romantic love. Incest being denied us, we must make do with second best.'[18]

This may help to explain not only the duality of the Rebecca figure – both desirable and wicked – as noted above, but also the odd mixture of characteristics which are manifested in du Maurier's heroines. The Rebecca figure reappears in several guises; she clearly informs the attractive but doomed Rachel in *My Cousin Rachel*, who makes the fatal error of wishing to run her own life, affairs, house and garden, and of treating both Ambrose and Philip as if they were, as indeed they are, impetuous, irresponsible, but lovable children. She is, as du Maurier confusingly describes her: 'A cold-blooded bitch ... you will never really know whether the woman is an angel or a devil.'[19]

In *The King's General* two heroines assume Rebecca-like features: Honor, with whom du Maurier identified,[20] and Gartred. From our first introduction to her – 'But Gartred. Those serpent's eyes beneath the red gold hair, that hard voluptuous mouth',[21] – we are reminded of the woman who 'gave you the feeling of a snake' according to simple-minded Ben.[22] Gartred indeed treats men cavalierly, lures Honor into the accident which cripples her, betrays the King's cause when it suits her, and is ultimately 'punished' by having her face scarred by one of her betrayed lovers. Nonetheless she glides through the interminable vicissitudes of the Civil War with her health and strength intact, still using her powers on hapless males while an early victim of her selfishness, Honor, writes the last words of her story. Honor herself is no angel – seduced, although it is not exactly clear how, by Gartred's equally arrogant and self-willed brother Sir Richard Grenvile *in an apple tree*. Honor is almost immediately 'punished' for this, and for rejecting parental and fraternal control, by being crippled in a riding accident. However, this accident saves her from the boredom of a conventional marriage and permits her to have an affair (of sorts, given her condition) with the dashing Richard Grenvile.

Grenvile would at first reading appear to be precisely the kind of hero, and lover, that Maxim sadly fails to be. He, it appears, is a true descendant of those monsters of depravity who terrify heroines in Gothic novels. He is arrogant, cruel and passionate. His only weakness seems to be his tenderness towards Honor. He is the kind of hero often held to be most women's ideal, although the fact that he allows his son to suffocate to death to facilitate his own escape might militate against him.

However, one cannot help but feel as one labours through this long tale not only that Richard is a one-dimensional character but also that he is not even the real hero of the novel, which is, in fact, the house, Menabilly (the house in which du Maurier herself lived for much of her adult life). Du Maurier herself was totally devoted to the place, at the expense of her marriage,[23] and in her detailed descriptions of its many sufferings, the real passion of Honor and du Maurier clearly merges.

In *Frenchman's Creek*, a novel du Maurier was never really happy about,[24] she succeeds to some extent in resolving the dualities implicit in her other heroes and heroines. Dona St Columb manages to combine in her own person those disparate elements presented as warring elsewhere. She is a happy and caring mother, but a bored wife and therefore a happy adulteress. For once, however, du Maurier resists the conventions and Dona triumphs, in her secret and sexually fulfilling escapade, not only over her somewhat unrealised and one-dimensional husband but also over the demon-figure of the novel, her husband's friend, Lord Rockingham.

Here, as in *Jamaica Inn*, du Maurier has divided the dominant male personae, rather than the female: Jean Pierre Benoit represents an acceptable version of maleness, as does Jem Merlyn in *Jamaica Inn*, whilst Rockingham, like the murderous Joss Merlyn, is violent and repulsive. Du Maurier has in fact returned to the conventional dichotomy of the Gothic novel: handsome but somewhat insipid hero versus sinister and interesting villain.

Of the two novels *Jamaica Inn* is undoubtedly the more effective. Its heroine, Mary Yellan, is, for du Maurier, an unusual heroine, in being working class, which perhaps enabled du Maurier to create in her a potent image of independent womanhood. Surrounded as she is by apparent villains (Joss, and for a time Jem) and real, but cleverly deceiving ones (Francis Davey), and by the brilliantly evoked setting of stormy moor and sea, wreckers and looters, 'romantic' Cornwall at its best, Mary triumphs, not only over villainy but over convention, choosing an uncertain life with the gipsy Jem over the respectable but dull alternatives: a life of service or a return to the farm at Helston. And to give her due credit, du Maurier does not romanticise Jem's life and prospects. Like Mary we have no doubts that her choice is dubious and fraught with dangers, emotional and economic. Margaret Forster gives a very different reading:

> and yet, at the end of the story, she cannot resist Jem's invitation to share his life, 'because I must'. She is a woman saved, a woman believing herself to be in love, but a woman beaten, left with no option, capitulating without joy on the basis of hope, a woman following the dictates of heart and body but not mind. It was a deeply pessimistic view of a woman's life.[25]

However, du Maurier can be more widely and variously interpreted. From Rebecca to Mary Yellan, du Maurier subverts our expectations. Characters doomed to conventional fates – Honor's marriage, Dona's staid familial roles – escape into adventures, into lives which challenge patriarchal role expectation. Whereas Stewart's novels reinforce patriarchy – marriage is the proper and desired fate of all her heroines – and embrace not only all the devices of the Gothic novel, but their shallowness of narrative structure and stereotypical characterisation, du Maurier's gift for the unusual in both character and setting informs the (often) slight freight of the actual story. What was in the Gothic novel mere decoration, and in *Jane Eyre* rather a contrived pathetic fallacy, becomes the hidden agenda of du Maurier's novels. For she, as her other novels, *The Scapegoat*, *Don't Look Now*, and *The House on the Strand* show, was fascinated by the strange and the unexpected – in character and experience. Ambiguity and uncertainty, the step that anyone might take into an unfamiliar and disturbing world, wherein one's expectations are challenged and even overthrown, these inform the unanswered questions left by the more apparently conventional novels. What *did* happen to Mrs Danvers? What became of Richard Grenvile, or Jean Pierre Benoit? Did Rachel poison Ambrose? It is because the answers are not implicit in their endings that du Maurier's novels are arguably so effective. Even the problem which still appears to remain with du Maurier's central love relationships may be argued as a strength. In order to survive, these relationships demand a degree of sacrifice – often, but not always, on the part of the heroine. The relationships of Jem and Mary, of Maxim and the second Mrs de Winter, of Dona and Lord St Columb, involve a denial of individuality and power so that they may succeed. More means less. It may be significant, in this regard, that du Maurier so often writes about *marriages*, not just about courtship and pursuit, and here too she differs from Mary Stewart. Marriage, as *My Cousin Rachel* shows most poignantly and dramatically, is not necessarily the hoped-for happy ending.

Finally, I would argue, the dichotomy Light perceives in the presentation of Rebecca and the second Mrs de Winter may in fact be du Maurier's strength. Women desire power and to be loved, to dominate and to be dominated. The second Mrs de Winter has, in the end, all the power she wants and all the love Maxim can give her, but is she happy? Unlike Brontë, du Maurier denies the reader the triumphalist happy ending, thus allowing her (or him) freedom from closure, freedom to speculate, although whether du Maurier would have approved of Susan Hill's sequel to *Rebecca*,[26] who knows? Du Maurier's novels, in their ambiguous even confusing portrayal of gender reflect, as Margaret Forster's biography reveals, a confused persona in their author.[27] And although she makes use of what is often, but in lesser writers, rejected as the paraphernalia of the Romantic/Gothic, fairytale tradition – skeletons in cupboards, sinister villains and threatening hags, haunted castles and windswept moors – she offers glimpses of the complexities of human nature and the peculiar power struggles and structures redolent of actual human relationships.

For a thorough and unquestioning reworking of both the Gothic/Romantic novel and the fairytale the reader should turn to Mary Stewart who adheres faithfully to the requirements of the genre, offering no subversion of expectations. A superficial reading of her novels, from *Madam Will You Talk?* (1957) to *Stormy Petrel* (1991), would suggest a package entirely satisfactory to the kind of female readership outlined in Janice Radway's 'Women Read the Romance':[28] women who look for a certain kind of pre-dictability of plot and characterisation and read to escape rather than be challenged. Stewart's novels, covering as they do a period of rapid change in the status of women, the rise of the feminist movement, the arrival of the Pill and Abortion Law reform and the Equal Opportunities Act, fail to register any of these. They conform, as Joanna Russ points out in her essay on the Gothic romance,[29] to a very specific pattern. Stewart's heroines, often apparently independent young women with jobs, self-sufficient and courageous, are emotionally and psychologically nineteenth-century Janes in search of Rochesters, Cinderellas waiting for princes, or, to use Brookner's terminology, tortoises triumphing over hares. Unlike du Maurier, Stewart has produced a formula novel which changes only its setting, never its patterns of character and plot. There is, however, a darker side, not always apparent at first reading: a much more explicit development and display of the sado-masochistic element inherent in male/female relationships in the Gothic/Romantic tradition. Stewart here, like du Maurier, borrows from *Jane Eyre*; the almost sadistic pleasure Rochester gets from allowing Jane to think he is about to marry Blanche Ingram is but the logical development of the Gothic aspect of his presentation which is evident in the first meeting in the dark and misty lane. Much of the contemporary reader's disquiet about Rochester's character stems, I would argue, from what appears to be Brontë's own ambivalence; on the one hand the novel and particularly that section of it dealing with Jane and Rochester's 'courtship' is heavily redolent of the Gothic: Thornfield's mad laughter, the appearance of its darkly sinister owner out of a misty winter's night, his boorishness and selfishness, the fire, the attack on Mason, not to mention the uncertainty in which Jane is kept regarding all aspects of the truth, about himself, Bertha, and Blanche; all of these combine with Jane's archetypal Gothic heroine situation as an unprotected orphan, unsure of her place in society or the world. On the other hand the novel has a highly moralistic, nineteenth-century element; this Gothic hero must be punished for his treatment of the heroine, first by losing her, then his sight and finally his arm. Only when he is maimed and properly subdued, when she can become the mistress of her former Master, can he be allowed to marry her.

This ambivalence allied with a considerable element of sado-masochism far more explicit than anything in Brontë, though common in the Gothic novel itself, pervades Stewart's novels; her heroines are often attracted by men whom they suspect of criminal acts; sexual attraction wars with a 1950s morality which prevents the author herself from achieving anything more than the simplistic 'happy ending' so inevitable in her stories. Love is a suitable topic for lengthy description; sex is reserved for villains and their doxies. Yet here again a peculiar element creeps in: often the heroine is forced into a voyeuristic position, experiencing the 'forbidden' pleasures at second hand. In both *My Brother Michael* (1959) and *Thunder on the Right* (1957) the revolted feelings of the heroine are recorded in a peculiarly titillating way. In the former, for example, the heroine, hiding from the murderous villain in a cave, is forced to overhear him first make love to his mistress – a rival for the hero's affections – and then kill her:

> I only heard one sound from her, and it was a little half-sigh, half whimper of pleasure. I'll swear it was of pleasure ...
>   And that is how Danielle Lascaux was murdered within twenty yards of me, and I never lifted a finger to help her.[30]

In *Thunder on the Right* the details of the kidnapping of the heroine's cousin following a car accident are rendered in even more explicit language, reminiscent of soft-core pornographic fantasy:

> She was lying on the grass in the torchlight with her hair spread out and her clothes half torn off her. She was lovely, and I wanted her ... So I picked her up and brought her here.[31]

What is interesting in both these novels, given the almost lip-smacking pleasure in describing sex and violence, is Stewart's determination to locate her fiction, by use of internal textual references and chapter epigraphs, within a *literary* context. Thus *My Brother Michael*, set in 1950s Greece, is not only about revenge but is heavy with Euripidean and Sophoclean references; *This Rough Magic* (1964) assumes its setting, Corfu, to have been the island of Shakespeare's *Tempest*, and uses Greek and Shakespearean parallels to inform text and plot. One can only speculate on Stewart's desire to impress the reader with her erudition; perhaps unfairly I believe that she simply wishes to have her cake and eat it: to appeal to both the baser and finer instincts of the reader at the same time, so the reader can feel this is not just escapist fantasy she is reading, but something which aspires to serious fiction.

The novel which is most self-consciously reflexive and interesting in this context, given the debt I believe Stewart owes Brontë, is *Nine Coaches Waiting* (1958). It also establishes the Stewart plot and character pattern. *Nine Coaches Waiting* is the story of Linda Martin, a 20-year-old half-French orphan, who takes the post of governess to a 9-year-old French count whose trustee and uncle has nefarious intentions concerning his life and property. This property is a chateau and estate near the French–Swiss border, suitably exotic and remote. There are, as usual, twin strands to the story: the primary narrative is really a thriller; Linda discovers the plot against Philippe and protects him by embarking on a thrilling and fraught escape to his 'safe' uncle's home. The secondary narrative is a romance: Linda inevitably falls in love with the villain's handsome son, Raoul, doubts his love for her, suspects – oh horror – that he is embroiled in the murder plot, and suffers angst and social opprobrium for having aspired above her station. In the denouement all ends happily: Jane gets her Rochester, after both of them have suffered just enough to deserve it, and the unhappy little boy finds a home with them. Linda, like all Stewart's heroines, is dazzlingly beautiful, resourceful and courageous, but her real career aspiration is to be a wife. For although many of Stewart's heroines have jobs, it is always implied if not explicit that these are but stepping-stones on the path to the true vocation – of wedded bliss.

Nine Coaches Waiting, too, in its presentation of the developing relationship between Raoul and Linda, has the usual Stewart elements of sado-masochism I referred to earlier:

> 'Then what's it to do with you what I do or who I see?'
> We were on the last slope of the zig-zag. The Cadillac jerked to a stop as the brakes were jammed on. Raoul de Valmy swung round on me.
> 'This,' he said, in a breathless, goaded undertone. He pulled me roughly towards him, and his mouth came down on mine.
> For a first kiss it was, I suppose, a fairly shattering experience. And certainly not such stuff as dreams are made on ... If Cinderella was out, so decidedly was Prince Charming ... Raoul de Valmy was simply an experienced man shaken momentarily out of self-control by anger and other emotions that were fairly easily recognisable even to me. I say 'even to me' because I discovered dismayingly soon that my own poise was a fairly egg-shell affair. For all my semi-sophistication I emerged from Raoul's embrace in a thoroughly shaken state which I assured myself was icy rage ...
> There was blood bitter-sweet on my tongue from a cut lip ... The whip flicked me again. Not only my face, my whole body burned.[32]

A further element in the sado-masochistic subtext, additional to the furtive enjoyment of pain inflicted by the lover – made more explicit elsewhere, as we shall see – is the enjoyment, guiltily but certainly experienced, of pain inflicted by the lover on the various villains threatening the heroine's life. Thus in *My Brother Michael*, the fight between Angelos and Simon, the hero, is *justified* because we know Angelos has murdered Simon's brother Michael (of the title), and a friendly artist, Nigel, not to mention Angelos's girlfriend Danielle (in the scene quoted above); he has, further, attempted to kill the heroine. The fight between the two men rages for *five* pages, before the heroine's horrified eyes. When Angelos is dead, she assumes Simon has done it to avenge his brother, but of course we know better, particularly if we are familiar with Stewart's other novels:

> 'My dear girl,' said Simon, 'surely you didn't imagine that I really killed him for Mick, did you?' ...
> 'He told me what the two of them had done to Nigel ... And then,' he said, 'there was you.'[33]

Like Raoul, Simon is the parfit knight, proving himself worthy of his lady by protecting her. This hand-to-hand conflict, although not always actually fatal for the villain, recurs as part of the plot-pattern in *The Gabriel Hounds* (1967), *The Moonspinners* (1962), *This Rough Magic* (1964), and even *Airs Above The Ground* (1965), where the heroine is already married to the hero, an unusual situation for a Stewart heroine; nonetheless Lewis behaves as if he too must prove himself in his lady's eyes, by torturing the villain who had earlier attacked and pursued her:

> 'I'll tell you anything! What do you want?'
> 'It can wait, ' said Lewis.
> And with the other's wrist in his grip, he dragged the arm forward, and began to force it out towards the stove where the kettle had stood.
> Sandor made no sound. It was Timothy who gasped, and I think I said: 'Lewis! NO!'
> But we might as well not have been there. It happened in slow motion. Slowly, sweating every inch of the way, Lewis forced the hand downwards. 'It was this hand, I believe?' [which had struck Vanessa] he said, and held it for a fraction of a second, no more, on the hot plate.
> Sandor screamed. Lewis pulled him away, dumped him unresisting into the nearest chair, and reached for the gun I was still holding ...
> 'Keep your hands to yourself after this,' said my husband, thinly.[34]

It is interesting that these novels were written during the 1960s, a time when women were beginning to assert their equality and independence. Stewart gives a nod only in this direction; Vanessa, for example, is a qualified veterinary surgeon, although there is no sign of her having practised since her marriage to the dashing Lewis. Stewart seems instead to reinforce conventional stereotypes of male/female characterisation and behaviour. Her view of what women are like, what they want from relationships, is strangely similar to the image of women purveyed in male popular fiction. Her presentation of violence is particularly significant in this respect. Stewart's novels become more violent, culminating in the quite horrifically violent *Touch Not the Cat* (1976). (Her two much later novels, *Thornyhold* (1988), and the more recent *Stormy Petrel* (1991), return to a less melodramatic, cosier 1950s atmosphere.)

The narratological function of this repeated pattern, in effect the archetypal Gothic situation of heroine threatened by fearsome villain, is to justify Stewart's deceitful presentation of her heroines. On the one hand they *appear* to be the epitome of modern womanhood, brave and independent; on the other they are as in need of a rescuing hero as any Radcliffe heroine. Stewart uses familiar devices to effect this *trompe-l'oeil*. With the solitary exception of Jennifer Silver in *Thunder on the Right*, Stewart uses a first person narrator, a well-known device for establishing reader sympathy and confidence. These heroine/narrators all establish their *bona fides* as initially fancy-free, financially independent (because they have jobs), and game for challenges such as ventures into foreign countries. Their courage and strong-mindedness is usually foregrounded by being contrasted with other, weaker women. They often loudly resent the heroes' protective attitudes towards them, and launch themselves quite foolhardily in lone pursuit of the villains. Violence on the part of these villains, first towards others weaker than the heroines – thus establishing them clearly as villains – and then towards the heroines themselves permits the heroines to revert to archetypal Gothic behaviour.

The archetypal Stewart heroine (subsequently modified slightly, possibly to suit the changing times), is Charity Selborne in *Madam Will You Talk?* (1955). Charity is spectacularly beautiful (according, of course, to others' testimony, since the book is narrated by Charity); she is a rich war widow with a penchant for fast cars (she was, of course, taught to drive by her dead husband, thus does Stewart ever undercut her heroines' abilities); she is accompanied on her vacation to a typical Stewart setting, Provence, by a less beautiful and much less active friend who acts as a foil. Charity becomes embroiled in a convoluted plot because she feels sorry (a very typical touch, this) for a young boy staying at the same hotel. This is a useful device, since it allows Stewart to establish her heroines' *bona fides* as *mothers* as well as lovers. Charity is at first confused as to the identity of the villain, and for a time mistakes the hero for him; as she is undoubtedly attracted to the hero, and of course he to her, this leads to emotional conflict. We are, however, given an insight into her feelings when the hero inadvertently bruises her arm when they first meet. Again and again we are reminded of those bruises, as she puts on a heavy bracelet (like a manacle?) to conceal them from her companion Louise, until at last she learns the truth about the hero, Richard Byron, and his feelings for her:

> He shifted his grip, and his eyes fell on my bruised wrist. For a second or two he stood with his head bent, staring at the ugly dark mark, then his mouth suddenly twisted, and he pulled me into his arms and kissed me.[35]

This 'enjoyment' of pain inflicted by the beloved appears even more explicitly in *This Rough Magic*; here the hero, Max Gale, believed by Lucy to be up to no good, grabs her 'brutally' in order to hide her from the actual villain of the novel; subsequently she discovers, not much to the reader's surprise, both that he is not a villain and that she loves him. On a drive the next day with the actual villain Lucy notices the bruises caused by the 'brutal' encounter:

> There was a curiously strong and secret pleasure, I had found, in speaking of him as 'Mr Gale' in the off-hand tones that Godfrey and Phyllida commonly used, as one might of a stranger to whom one is under an obligation, but whom one hardly considers enough to like or dislike. Once, as I had mentioned his name in passing, my eye, downcast, caught the faint mark of a bruise on my arm. The secret thrill of pleasure that ran up my spine startled me a little; I slipped my other hand over the mark to hide it, and found it cupping the flesh as if it were his, and not my own. I looked away, out of the car, and made some random remark about the scenery.[36]

Similar 'brutality' on the part of the villain, in both *Madam Will You Talk?* and *This Rough Magic* is not regarded as quite so appealing, however, and this is made clear by the identification of the villain in both novels, and elsewhere, as not only truly evil but representative of a lower class of being than the hero; Godfrey's threat to Lucy's life and honour, for example, in *This Rough Magic* is expressed in such coarse terms that it reveals his true nature to her: 'It was like acid spilling over a polished surface, to show the stripped wood, coarse and ugly.'[37] And in *Madam Will You Talk?* Charity sees the villain, whom she once took to be the hero, for what he is:

> Now that I knew, oh, yes, now that I knew, it was plain to see, the glint of amusement below the insolent lids, the arrogant tilt of the chin, the whole formidable confidence of the man. And I was aware again, sharply, of the impression of excitement that I had received before: somehow, it was there, banked and blazing, under the smoothly handsome exterior: the faint gleam of sweat over his cheekbones betrayed it, the nostrils that flared to a quicker breathing above a rigid upper lip, the hands, too tight upon the wheel. Murderer's hands.
>
> The dim road hurtled towards us. A village, a huddle of houses flickered by like ghosts. Ahead two eyes gleamed: they stared, then darted like fireflies as the rabbit turned to run. Paul Very gave a little laugh, and deliberately thrust down his foot. I heard the rabbit squeal as we hit it ... Paul Very laughed once more.[38]

Identifying features of Stewart villains include ill-treatment of animals, and pretending to a class to which they do not belong. (No right-thinking male could wantonly kill a dolphin (Godfrey in *This Rough Magic*) or a rabbit, as Paul Very does here). Class is also a convenient way of identifying villainesses; Stewart allows them to be attractive but immoral; unlike her chaste heroines they sleep with the villains and attempt to seduce the heroes. They always come to a bad end; like Danielle Lascaux in *My Brother Michael*, Loraine Bristol in *Madam Will You Talk?* and Halide in *The Gabriel Hounds*, they die at the hands of their masters.

Class is far more of a problem for Stewart than it is for du Maurier. Stewart after all is writing in a time when British society has become much less hierarchical, and in *Touch Not the Cat* she makes an effort to recognise this. Her heroine, Bryony Ashley, although the daughter of an old aristocratic family, is so poor that she must work for her living, can only afford a Lambretta and, most egalitarian of all, discovers that her 'secret' lover, with whom she is in telepathic touch, is the gardener's son Rob Grainger and not, as she had believed, one of her aristocratic cousins. The way in which Rob's working-classness is revealed to us is interesting, given Stewart's use in earlier novels of oral gratification to indicate the recognition of a relationship. In *Madam Will You Talk?* for example, the scene in which Charity submits to Richard is preceded by one in which she allows him to give her a sumptuous meal:

> I obeyed him, and lay back against the deep cushions with my eyes closed, letting my body relax utterly to the creeping warmth of the drink and the smell of food and wine and flowers. My bones seemed to have melted, and I was queerly content to lie back against the yielding velvet, with the soft lights against my eyelids, and do nothing, think of nothing. I was quiet and utterly passive, and the awful beginnings of hysteria were checked ... there were anchovies and tiny gleaming silver fish in red sauce, and savoury butter in curled strips of fresh lettuce; there were caviare and tomato and olives green and black, and small golden-brown fowl bursting with truffles and flanked by tiny peas, then a froth of ice and whipped cream dashed with kirsch, and the smooth caress of the wine through it all ...[39]

Compare this with Bryony's homecoming meal with Rob:

> I got the grill going, and laid the sausages and tomatoes to cook while Rob took things from drawers and cupboards, and neat-handed for all his size, laid the extra place and sliced bread and tipped another helping of frozen chips into the frying basket.[40]

Rob is truly a New Man, but Stewart cannot quite abandon herself to the ethos of the 1970s. Rob will not sleep with Bryony before they are married and turns out anyway to be the legitimate heir to Ashley Court, an aristocrat after all. In a revealing scene when her life is in danger, what really concerns Bryony is that her aristocratic and murderous cousins believe her to be *sleeping* with the gardener's boy. Bryony is as bourgeois and narrow-minded as Linda in *Nine Coaches Waiting*; what other people will think matters almost more than anything else. In this Stewart is a true descendant of the nineteenth century, although her plots and characters ultimately owe more to Frances Hodgson Burnett than to the Brontës.

I have spent some time on a discussion of Stewart's novels because their structure, style and characterisation, I feel, inform subsequent texts which I am to analyse. Both Mills & Boon novels and those of Conran, Collins etc use many of her tried and therefore trusted techniques. Stewart's novels are redeemed from total identification with these subsequent texts by her use of the detective story paradigm, a device forbidden to Mills & Boon writers. Stewart's narrative style, although tending to the melodramatic especially where dialogue is concerned, at least makes use of setting description to provide atmosphere, whereas Mills & Boon novels, although nominally set in exotic locations, could as well be set in Surbiton. But there is no doubt that despite Stewart's valiant efforts to suggest, by means of chapter epigraphs and internal textual references to Greek and Renaissance literature, that her novels should properly be seen as *literary* rather than popular texts, Joanna Russ's description of the appeal of the modern Gothic in general seems to apply only too readily to Stewart:

1. If I must be passive, I might as well make the most of it.
2. If I must suffer, I will do so spectacularly and luxuriously.
3. I really want to get in on those jewel-smugglings and murders and exciting stuff.
4. If my man treats me badly, that's because he's masculine, not because he's bad. There are bad men and good men; the problem is simply telling which is which. There are bad women and good women; I'm not a bad (read: sexual, aggressive) woman.
5. Conventionally masculine men are good men (even if they treat me badly) and conventionally feminine women are good women. This makes behavior very easy to judge. It also validates conventional sex roles.
6. I am bored and therefore make much of trifles.
7. *Something* is trying to hurt me and tear me down – but I don't know what it is. I suspect it's my man, or men in general, but that's an unthinkable thought.
8. Nobody respects me except when they're sexually attracted to me or benefiting from my selflessness (read: treating me as a convenience).
    CONCLUSION: I will go read another Gothic novel.[41]

In other words, Stewart's novels achieve the same effect on the reader as a Mills & Boon novel: they are as addictive and as challenging as a box of chocolates. In terms of Cawelti's criteria cited in the Introduction du Maurier can properly be described as being inventive. She uses the devices of the fairytale and the Gothic to explore the parameters of possible female roles; to challenge accepted perceptions and interpretations. Stewart allows the devices of Ann Radcliffe to operate unchallenged and virtually unchanged. Her influence, sado-masochism included, rather than du Maurier's, alas, informs much of twentieth-century popular fiction by women.

However, before looking at her obvious successors, let us look at writers in two apparently different genres: the 'comedy of manners' and the detective story, to see if generic writing can escape the heavy and pervasive influence of the nineteenth-century fairy and Gothic tale.

2

Manners Makyth (Wo)Man: The Novels of Anita Brookner and Barbara Pym

Anita Brookner is carrying on undeterred. She is setting out her old archetypes in a slightly different arrangement, and they are as 'timeless' as any in a more hot-blooded romance.[1]

This comment, from a review of Brookner's novel *Family Values* (1993), offers a hint as to why we might well choose to see her as having fallen, like Stewart, into the trap of writing formula novels. Another review, of her 1992 novel *Fraud*, suggests a similar perception:

> Anita Brookner's twelfth novel is a terrifying, hilarious, frantically paced comedy-thriller, centred on the adventures of two down-at-heel drag queens who are taken hostage by a serial killer and forced to accompany him at knifepoint on a headlong flight from the police through the clubs, brothels and strip-joints of Berlin's notorious red light district.
> Well, we must all be allowed our little fantasies.[2]

One cannot but agree with the reviewer, Jonathan Coe, and find the title of this novel perhaps only too apt a word to describe what Brookner has been doing to her large readership over a period of years, ever since she won the Booker prize with *Hotel Du Lac* in 1984. This novel, as it happens, does have a deservingly interesting narrative structure which appears to expose the life-limiting nature of an existence as a romantic novelist. Its heroine, a first-person narrator named Edith Hope is, of course, not to be confused with Anita Brookner; indeed in a BBC interview consequent upon the public interest in the then shortlisted novel, Brookner made much of the fact that by birth she could not belong to the society explored and exposed in the novel, rejecting attempts to relate her to the Jane Austen school of fiction, stating very firmly what has become all too evident in her subsequent writing, her sense of being an outsider, an alien observing the minutiae of the manners of the tribe, *not* the ironic member of the tribe that Austen undoubtedly was.

And yet it is also certainly the case that Austen is exactly the novelist Brookner reminds us of, as does Barbara Pym. Both give detailed portrayals of the intimate lives of a few select characters whose pursuit of happiness, especially in terms of relationships, whether with members of the opposite sex or their parents, is beset with difficulty and is ultimately a failure. Coe's review continues:

> Of course one doesn't stop to wonder, when picking up a new Brookner novel, what it is going to be 'about'. It will be about lonely women living in South Kensington; it will be about the quiet victories of the woman of integrity over the emotional predator; it will be about the bonds of dependence formed between parent and child, and how these will inevitably have a distorting effect on future romantic relationships.[3]

The 'victories' he refers to are usually of a Pyrrhic nature; the celebration, if one can call it that, takes place within the heroine's mind, as she ruefully bends her head – a favourite Brooknerism – to the task in hand. Novel after novel ends in the same bathetic way:

> Doctor Weiss returned her lecture notes to their file, plugged in her electric kettle, and made herself a cup of coffee ... Then she reached for a sheet of paper. Dear Ned, she wrote, dear Ned, it is so long since we met ... Will you come to dinner next week or the week after? It will have to be either Wednesday or Thursday as the weekends are eroded at either end by my father. He is very old now and since my mother's death relies on my company rather heavily. And of course you must be busy yourself. Do let me know when we can meet. P. S. The section on Eugenie Grandet has turned out rather longer than expected. Do you think anyone will notice?[4]

> They took their places at the table, Maurice and Miss Fairchild at either end. I lacked the information, thought Kitty, trying to control her trembling hands. Quite simply, I lacked the information. She had the impression of having been sent right back to the beginning of a game she thought she had been playing according to the rules. And there was the rest of the evening to be got through ...[5]

Making her way silently along the thick carpet, anxious not to awaken or alarm the sleeping guests, she was just in time to see Jennifer's door open and Mr Neville, in his dressing gown, emerge ...

Of course, she thought. Of course ...

And back in her room she realized how little surprised she was ...

She saw her father's patient face. Think again, Edith. You have made a false equation ...[6]

That evening Harriet, standing at the window, saw the sun descend majestically into the lake. Turning, she surveyed the empty room. My life, she thought, an empty room. But she felt no pain, felt in fact the cautious onset of some kind of release. Vividly, she caught sight of Immy's [her daughter, killed in a horrific car accident long ago] face. She drew in a deep breath, laughed. There it was again, Immy's face as it had always been. She laughed again, at the image of Immy's laughing face. Sinking on to the sofa she let the tears rain down. Never again to lack for company. All will be as before, she thought, as she wept in gratitude. When my little girl was young.[7]

In the last example, of course, we know that Harriet's 'little girl' was never what Harriet thought of her: that this 'vision' is no more and no less illusory than everything else in Harriet's life. And this seems to be Brookner's main theme and technique: her heroines are unaware and we are fully informed of the extent of the knowledge and understanding that they lack. (Lewis Percy, Brookner's sole hero to date, is simply a male version of the recurring pattern.) In her earlier novels, however, she seemed to promise much more.

In the early novels, especially *A Start in Life* and *Providence*, there was, it seemed, a sense of irony, even humour; the first line of *A Start in Life* has an almost Austen-like ring about it: 'Dr Weiss, at forty, knew that her life had been ruined by literature.'[8] And Brookner in the BBC interview mentioned earlier admitted two recurrent patterns in her novels: a Cinderella-reversal story and a moral education story. Many of her heroines and also her hero Lewis Percy are interested or even expert in French literature; the notion therefore of an 'education sentimentale' suggests a nineteenth-century theme applied to twentieth-century life. But Brookner ultimately lacks French detachment. True, as she says, we are shown heroines who feel 'left out' and want to be 'let in' to what they perceive to be the adult world; they expect a 'stroke of luck' which never comes; they are as Edith Hope describes them in *Hotel Du Lac*:

> Women prefer the old myths ... They want to believe that they are going to be discovered, looking their best, behind closed doors, just when they thought that all was lost, by a man who has battled across continents, abandoning whatever he may have had in his in-tray, to reclaim them.[9]

In that sense her stories reverse the Cinderella myth. But are they stories of 'moral education'? Certainly they have an almost Aristotelian moment of peripety or reversal; a moment which one might expect to lead also to an Aristotelian knowledge of the self. But this is not what happens; the heroine having encountered 'the facts of life [which] are too terrible to go into [Edith Hope's] kind of fiction',[10] retreats into familiar structures of being, hiding her head tortoise-like, to use another 'Hope' term. Brookner's heroines are always, even despite marriage, virginal, adolescent, unable to sustain mature relationships with other adults, especially males. And the problem is that we are not apparently allowed, as we might be in a French novel, to find them risible; we are supposed to pity them: to see them as sad victims whom the rich pageant of life has passed by.

One can see here *Hotel Du Lac* as a pivotal and illuminating novel. It is certainly one of Brookner's best and has fewer of those irritatingly unconvincing working-class stereotypes than her other, especially later, novels. It also uses as its focalising persona – to use Rimmon-Kenan's useful term[11] – a romantic novelist, 'totemistically-named' (as Brookner admitted in her BBC interview) Edith Hope, who writes as Vanessa Wilde – a name with interesting connotations. Edith's own life is archetypal Brookner; she is the child of emigré parents, like Brookner herself; she has had and has in the novel an unsatisfactory love-life; she sees herself as an observer of others, a somewhat self-congratulatory one at that:

> I have been too harsh on women, she thought, because I understand them better than I understand men. I know their watchfulness, their patience, their need to advertise themselves as successful. Their need never to admit to a failure.[12]

But, and this is an irony heavily underlined by Brookner, Edith does not understand them; she stereotypes them and when she guesses at them, cannot even get their ages right, and she understands herself least of all. It is uncertain what we are supposed to feel at the end of the novel. Is Edith too happy in her unhappy state ever to change it? Is she happy to be an escapist writer of old-fashioned fiction that her publisher is getting bored with? Does she prefer the half-life of being David's mistress to a full-time commitment to any other man? Are we meant to feel a kind of detached compassion for such a self-deluding character? That, it seems to me, is the logical deduction to make from the deliberate paralleling of Edith's real life and the kind of romantic fiction she writes. However, in the light of Brookner's subsequent novels and a succession of such characters, one cannot but suspect that we are meant to feel that she is to be sympathised with: that it is the rest of the characters and their ways of life which are wrong, that we are meant to see the Edith Hope persona embattled against a hostile world. However, this is not the kind of heroic message which is conveyed by the text to this reader with any degree of success. Brookner works too hard to detach 'story' from 'text' (to use Genette's terminology).

Throughout *Hotel Du Lac* we see Brookner as superior to Edith. Brookner uses a variety of narrative devices to create suspense and to impel the reader on; she sets up a variety of male and female characters, raises the issues of anorexia, the solitariness of old age, the predatoriness of men and the vulnerability of her own particular heroine. One can see why the novel won the Booker Prize. However, neither the structural innovations nor the potentially feminist issues are developed or addressed in subsequent novels. For the reader who hopes for a true Cinderella story and its comforting happy ending there is only anti-climax; for the reader aware, as Brookner does not seem to be, of the possibilities of feminist closure there is only disappointment.

Perhaps Brookner's message, if she has one, is that life, for her kind of heroine, or hero, is ultimately unfulfilling. One is dragged down by one's relatives, drawn into unsatisfactory relationships, let down by one's friends and one's lovers. But her characters are sad things, concerned with dreams and superficialities. Brookner is not like Jane Austen, not because she comes from the 'marginal' emigré world of the alien in English society – such a background could have offered an alternative richness of cultural experience – but because she observes and therefore creates only one-dimensional characters. There is no moral depth to her heroines; they appear incapable of learning from their experiences. What seemed like wit and irony in the early novels is presented increasingly as incontrovertible truth in the more recent novels. Like Edith Hope, Brookner has found her formula, and why should she change it? Every year another discourse upon vulnerability comes out and although Jan Dalley, in her review of *Fraud*, begins by saying:

> The desire to kick Anita Brookner's heroines is always strong, and Anna Durrant, the latest in the long line of Brookner's tight-lipped, clean-fingered women, is no exception. The floppy masochism with which she allows her not-very-sick mother to commandeer her life, and the exquisite by-ways of her loneliness after her mother's death are all the more irritating for being compounded of a good deal of laziness and self-aggrandisement: the rest of us, coarse-grained creatures, are just not good enough for her.[13]

Yet still there is the review; there is the book on the bestseller lists and stands. Brookner gives us in detail the story of some character who might have happily, or more likely unhappily, inhabited a corner in a room in a Dostoevsky novel, provided an opportunity for an abrasive comment in a Balzac novel. Reading Brookner one might think the whole Feminist movement had never occurred, and one begins to think the outrageousness of a Sally Beauman or the thorough-going romantic escapism of a Mary Stewart would satisfy the reader more effectively. With Brookner what you see is what you get: misery that is never quite tragedy; an over-reliance on caricature in the background characters; and a heroine who has become an all-too-familiar stereotype – a timid, virginal dreamer of not-very-interesting dreams, a woman who can apparently endure the death of loved ones, the loss of love and the demise of hope without ever changing or learning. Brookner has created a 'formula' which has proved popular; although at first sight, with her continual references to literature and the evident erudition of her heroines and hero, she would seem to be making an appeal to a *literary* rather than simply literate readership; to the kind of women represented in her heroine-figures in fact, yet in terms of John G Cawelti's 'concept of formula in popular culture' as referred to in the Introduction:

> conventions are elements which are known to both the creator and his audience beforehand – they consist of things like favorite plots, stereotyped characters, accepted ideas, commonly known metaphors and other linguistic devices, etc ...

conventions represent familiar shared images and meanings and they assert an ongoing continuity of values; inventions confront us with a new perception or meaning which we have not realized before.[14]

Brookner could be said in her early and arguably wittier novels to give her reader a sense of 'invention', but in her later and certainly most recent novels, she has come to offer us 'conventions'. Again *Hotel Du Lac* is illuminating; in a long passage describing her work Edith Hope outlines what has in a sense become the 'hidden agenda' or 'formula' of Brookner's own fiction:

> And what is the most potent myth of all? ... The tortoise and the hare ... People love this one, especially women. Now you will notice ... that in my books it is the mouse-like unassuming girl who gets the hero, while the scornful temptress with whom he has had a stormy affair retreats baffled from the fray, never to return. The tortoise wins every time. This is a lie of course ... in real life, of course, it is the hare who wins. Every time. Look around you. And in any case it is my contention that Aesop was writing for the tortoise market.
> Axiomatically ... Hares have no time to read. They are too busy winning the game. The propaganda goes all the other way, but only because it is the tortoise who is in need of consolation. Like the meek who are going to inherit the earth.[15]

Here Brookner is inviting us through her use of an observer, Harold, to see Edith in a positive, i.e. self-knowing light, yet later on, in a letter to her lover, Edith admits:

> You thought, perhaps, like my publisher, and my agent, who are always trying to get me to bring my books up to date and make them sexier and more exciting, that I wrote my stories with that mixture of satire and cynical detachment that is thought to become the modern writer in this field. You were wrong. I believed every word I wrote. And I still do, even though I realize now that none of it can ever come true for me.[16]

In what is perhaps an even more revealing passage, in conversation with the anorexic Monica, who has just accused her of 'being a bit thick', in terms of her observation of human nature, Edith says:

'It occurs to me ... that some women close ranks because they hate men and fear them. Oh, I know that this is obvious. What I'm really trying to say is that I dread such women's attempts to recruit me, to make me their accomplice. I'm not talking about the feminists. I can understand their position, although I'm not all that sympathetic to it. I'm talking about the ultra-feminine. I'm talking about the complacent consumers of men with their complicated but unwritten rules of what is due to them. Treats. Indulgences. Privileges. The right to make illogical fusses. The cult of themselves. Such women strike me as dishonourable. And terrifying. I think perhaps that men are an easier target. I think perhaps the feminists should take a fresh look at the situation.'

She stopped. What she was trying to say, although deeply felt, did not make much sense ...[17]

When *Hotel Du Lac* was published, won the Booker Prize, and was turned into a TV play starring Anna Massey, it was possible to see Edith Hope as a deluded being, exposed in all her limitedness, and to believe her creator a more superior and *knowing* being. Subsequently, however, this view, the limited and rather confused Edith Hope view, of feminists, of worldly-wise women and of men as their hapless victims as well as exploiters of the 'tortoise' women, has become the 'formula' of a Brookner novel. Additionally characterisation of minor figures has become more and more formulaic; Harriet's mother and father in *A Closed Eye* are much less effective, despite their much fuller portrayal, than those briefly described in *Hotel Du Lac*. The very readership the early Brookner clearly aimed at is becoming, as the two reviews cited earlier indicate, weary of Brookner's own limitations. However, Brookner has been fortunate in her early and continued success, deserved or not, compared with the other writer to be discussed in this chapter: Barbara Pym.

It is now a part of literary mythology that Pym, despite an early success with her first six novels, from *Some Tame Gazelle* (1950) to *No Fond Return of Love* (1961), suffered a self-confessedly humiliating rejection of her subsequent work, until her 'cause', as it were, was taken up by Philip Larkin, who in 1977, after almost a decade of personal encouragement of Pym, wrote in the *Times Literary Supplement*, that she was 'an underrated novelist'.[18] Pym's letters and notebooks, now published as *A Very Private Eye* (1984), together with *A Lot to Ask: A Life of Barbara Pym*, by Hazel Holt, (a friend and literary executrix) (1990), reveal a woman who from her youth wanted to be *recognised* as a writer. The recognition came almost too late for Pym, who died of cancer in 1980, but with articles and books about her work appearing now, especially in America, her claims would seem to have been gratifyingly realised. The almost mystifying appeal of Pym's novels to an *American* readership is partially explained by the title of one of these American critiques: *The World of Barbara Pym* by Janice Rossen.[19]

It is precisely this *world* created by Pym, of English middle-classness, of the 'excellent women' who never marry and find a curious kind of fulfilment, not at all religious in nature, in their involvement with the Anglican Church, which has the appeal of 'quaintness' so beloved of Americans. Sometimes Pym's heroines are married, like Wilmet Forsyth in *A Glass of Blessings* (1958) but, as with Brookner's heroines, marriage as a state is not always convincingly rendered. It is the other relationships that are the more interesting and effectively created; the network of relationships built up, often around a church, as in *A Glass of Blessings*, or in the 'village'-like structure of a London neighbourhood, as in *The Sweet Dove Died*, written in 1963, but not published until 1978, or the actual village setting of perhaps her most famous *roman-à-clef*, *Some Tame Gazelle*, largely written before and in the early years of the war, although revised and actually published in 1950, or interestingly, her last novel, *A Few Green Leaves* (1980). This last is particularly significant since it has as its heroine a young anthropologist who applies her techniques to a detailed observation of the quirks of human nature, much as Pym herself applied both her natural curiosity and her experience of working for anthropologists.

Reading Pym's letters and Holt's biography one cannot help being struck by the closeness of a great deal of Pym's own life-experiences to the lives revealed in her novels. An unhappy love affair at Oxford led, famously, to *Some Tame Gazelle*; a much later involvement with a much younger man informed *The Sweet Dove Died*; her experience of office life led to *Quartet in Autumn* (1977). Unlike Brookner, and probably because Pym's writing spanned her whole adult life, Pym's novels reflect both the changing perceptions of an ageing woman and a changing England: the village of *A Few Green Leaves* no longer recognises the Anglican Church as its centre, people going rather to the doctor than to the vicar for advice. Perhaps it is Pym, rather than Brookner, who deserves the comparison with Jane Austen?

Certainly Pym displays more of that almost wicked ironic wit which we associate with Austen, whether it be in her private but now published notebooks, or in the novels themselves:

> There were people clustering round it [Virginia Water] ... a man and two small boys accompanied by Mum and perhaps Gran in white Orlon cardigans, with the bright floral prints of their dresses showing through them. How did such people manage to get time off in the week? Leonora wondered.[20]

> Although from her upbringing it might have been thought that 'visiting the sick' would be part of her daily life she had hardly ever – thanks to the Welfare State – had to perform this duty.[21]

This kind of comment upon character combined with a sharp eye for the details of contemporary life is what Pym has most clearly in common with her ardent fan Philip Larkin. His recently published letters reveal also a 'cattiness' which Pym has herself, as revealed in this rather bitter comment on the critical response to *The Sweet Dove Died* shows:

> What is wrong with being obsessed with trivia? Some have criticised *The Sweet Dove* for this. What are the minds of my critics filled with? What *nobler* and more worthwhile things?[22]

A similar sharpness can be found in her characters, from her first to her last novel:

> The new curate seemed quite a nice young man, but what a pity it was that his combinations showed, tucked carelessly into his socks, when he sat down.[23]

> Beatrix ... found herself thinking that Emma could have made herself more attractive. She was getting a little too old for the modish drabness and wispiness so fashionable today. Surely a dress of a prettier colour and some attempt at a hair style ... might have made the evening more successful? It wasn't as if Emma had ever produced anything that could justify such high-minded dowdiness.[24]

According to Janice Rossen: 'Pym seems not only sincerely unhappy to hear her name linked with that of Austen, but horrifed.'[25] As of course did Brookner in the broadcast interview cited earlier. Perhaps the references by critics to Austen are simply a shorthand, a way of identifying authors who seem to them to be imitating Austen in addressing what seem to them to be similar kinds of audience using similar stories, settings and characters, for what we can expect from reading the work of these two writers, a way of indicating that their literary forebear is not a Brontë, that they are essentially *not* romantic novelists. But are they then in that line of descent I discussed in the Introduction, along with George Eliot and Elizabeth Gaskell? I think not. Superficially they would appear to have some Austen-like things in common; they write about small groups of interacting people; they are concerned with unrequited and often risibly hopeless love; neither is particularly effective when writing about the working classes; both appear to have a firm moral view about proper behaviour. But there I feel the similarity ends. Neither writer manages to produce heroes and heroines as lively and intelligent as Austen, and neither allows the depth of personal awareness to develop in their heroines by the end of the novels that Austen makes manifest. Both of them have invited this comparison by their use of terms like 'gentlewomen', and their use of irony.

However, if we abandon the Austen paradigm and ignore the tendency in both writers to draw attention self-consciously to the fact that they are not rewriting *Jane Eyre*, is there a genre to which they both belong that makes comparison of them both in the same chapter useful rather than invidious? It is my contention that there is; it is a genre which owes much to Ivy Compton Burnett, a favourite with Pym, and to which the recent novels of Joanna Trollope – a writer often compared over-generously with Pym – belong. It is a genre marked as much by the style of characters, their failures and inadequacies, as by any actual plot. Indeed, plot is usually the least important element in either a Brookner or a Pym story. With Pym particularly the novels end rather than come to any kind of dramatic conclusion; and life, we suppose, goes on.

Where Pym undoubtedly scores over Brookner, apart from her often mordant wit, is, as I said earlier, in the way in which her novels have traced a changing England, as well as in the way in which her detachment allows the reader to observe and possibly pity her characters rather than, as with Brookner, feel *compelled* to sympathise with what are ultimately monsters of egocentricity.

There is perceptibly a change in Pym's style, approach and vision of the England (and it *is* England, not Britain) that forms the background to her novels; indeed it might be said that England and a particular kind of Englishness forms a major part of the storyline of her novels. Her first novel, *Some Tame Gazelle*[26] was written as both a *roman-à-clef* – and to be understood as such by her fellow students at Oxford – and what is almost a caricature of a Jane Austen/Ivy Compton Burnett kind of novel: that is, much is owed to Austen in the deliberate limiting of the size of the observed community, and much is owed to Compton Burnett in the style and kinds of verbal exchange. Such is the extreme, there is almost caricatured behaviour of the female characters in particular, echoes of Agatha Christie's Miss Marple and Saint Mary Mead in the details of single ladies' lives and their involvement with the church. In fact it is a peculiarly elderly kind of novel for a young Oxford graduate to have written and is redolent of a past time, when servants and sewing women were common features in middle-class households. It has, in its portrayal of the comfortable relationship between the two sisters, Belinda and Harriet, a strange prescience about the retired lives the two Pym sisters would lead in the 1970s. At the heart of the novel is Belinda's unrequited but continuing love for Henry Hoccleve, a relationship based, as are most of the 'love' relationships in Pym's novels, on her own unrequited love for Henry Harvey, whom she continued to care for, and indeed spent 'Weekend Breaks' with in his and her retirement years. This love, unrequited or not, is portrayed as a *comfortable* kind of emotion rather than unhappy or disturbing; placidity and acceptance indeed marks Belinda's character:

> 'I feel that I have been lacking in manners for not offering it sooner,' said Belinda, quite sincerely, thus taking upon herself the blame for all the little frictions of the evening. But it was so obvious that women should take the blame, it was both the better and the easier part ...[27]

This is perhaps a tribute to Pym, since her notebooks reveal her intense unhappiness at Henry's unexpected marriage. Later novels, however, not written primarily for a coterie, are more honest in their perceptions; the tendency of men to take women for granted, as housekeepers, providers of comfort and consolation, amanuenses and general dogsbodies, is portrayed, largely without any apparent malice, throughout her novels. Even in her last, *A Few Green Leaves*, the supposedly liberated Emma feels sorry for the dreadful Graham and the pathetic Tom, who feels so deprived of his rightful female support-system when his sister goes to live with an old school-friend that he *advertises* his needs in the parish magazine! Before we know where we are, and *despite* Emma's awareness of her own folly, she is trotting through the woods with food for Graham and inviting the hapless Tom for an evening meal. Janice Rossen makes an interesting point about this:

> Like all writers, Pym regarded fiction as a means of saying something for others about her situation, of communicating her vision, as all artists do – but the interesting thing in Pym's work is that she seems so fastidious and detached from her subject-matter, and yet at the same time it is highly autobiographical ...
> The irony (and excellence) of Pym's work lies precisely here. For writing is a means of quiet, satisfactory revenge; a matter of satirising oneself, yet also of exposing the vagaries and absurdities of others, particularly men.[28]

This does however, like Rossen's whole approach, seem uncritical and a little over-generous. Pym herself seems more aware of a tension at the heart of her work between what she says and what she feels:

> Why is it that *men* find my books so sad? Women don't particularly. Perhaps they (men) have a slight guilt feeling that this is what they do to us, and yet really it isn't as bad as all that.[29]

The tension is the more poignant for Pym's dependence on *men* for support; without the championship of Philip Larkin and Lord David Cecil, and without Bob Smith's own influential essay on her in *Ariel* in 1971,[30] entitled, tellingly 'How Pleasant to Know Miss Pym', with all the connotations of the misquotation and the appellation 'Miss', Pym's novels would have remained out of print and perhaps her last two, *A Few Green Leaves* and *Quartet In Autumn*, unwritten. Throughout her personal and working life Pym moved in a world peopled by men like the ones portrayed in her novels, charming, feckless, inadequate, but always feeling themselves to be superior to women. It is not surprising that Pym's novels centre on women who are manipulated, exploited, condescended to; who are unlucky or misled in love; who misread men's intentions yet always seem to blame themselves for the failure of any relationship. This pattern recurs in characters as disparate in status and age as Wilmet in *A Glass of Blessings*, Ianthe in *An Unsuitable Attachment*, Letty in *Quartet in Autumn* and

Emma in *A Few Green Leaves*; these characters with their over-sensitive awareness of their own failings and their inability to cope with the male-dominated world in which they perceive themselves as living manifest what could be called archetypal Pym characteristics and behaviour:

> 'Oh', I was a little cast down. 'Is that how I am – cool and dignified? I don't mind being thought elegant, of course – but cool and dignified. It doesn't sound very lovable.'
> 'Lovable? Is that how you want to be?' He sounded surprised.
> 'I should have thought everyone did on this sort of afternoon', I said, rather at a loss. It was evident that his mood did not quite match mine, and that I should have to – as women nearly always must – damp down my own exuberant happiness until we were more nearly in sympathy.
> 'Wilmet, what's the matter with you? You're talking like one of the cheaper women's magazines.' Piers' tone was rather petulant.
> Love is the cheapest of all emotions, I thought; or such a universal one that it makes one talk like a cheap magazine. What, indeed, was the matter with me?[31]

What *is* the matter with Wilmet is that she fancies herself in love with Piers, who, it is clear to us, is not in the least interested in women at all; instead of perceiving this obvious truth, Wilmet wastes her time and emotions on adjusting herself to fit in with the moods of a fantasised lover.

In *An Unsuitable Attachment* Ianthe finds *herself* being misread, this time by a woman, but note the self-reflexive acceptance of the comments:

> 'You seem to me to be somehow *destined* not to marry', [Sophie] went on, perhaps too enthusiastically. 'I think you'll grow into one of those splendid spinsters – oh, don't think I mean it nastily or cattily – who are pillars of the church and whom the church certainly couldn't do without.'
> Ianthe was silent, as well she might be before this daunting description. Yet until lately she too had seen herself like this.[32]

Self-effacing, self-reflexive thoughts are features common to the Pym heroine:

Letty felt like a governess in a Victorian novel arriving at a new post, but there would be no children here and no prospect of a romantic attachment to the widower master of the house or a handsome son of the family. Her own particular situation had hardly existed in the past, for now it was the unattached working woman, the single 'business lady' of the advertisements, who was most likely to arrive in the house of strangers.[33]

This self-conscious reference to *not* being a Jane Eyre is typical of the Pym heroine. More poignant, because more individual and more relevant to Pym herself, is the reflection on the work Letty and Marcia did before they retired:

The activities of their department seemed to be shrouded in mystery – something to do with records or filing, it was thought, nobody knew for certain, but it was evidently 'women's work', the kind of thing that could easily be replaced by a computer. The most significant thing about it was that nobody was replacing them, indeed the whole department was being phased out.[34]

The sadness here is the implication that all that they have done is rendered null and meaningless. If, as Letty reflects, all her life has been is her work, now that too is a void.

Reviews of *A Quartet in Autumn* referred to its sombre tone, and despite the move of her personae back to the countryside of her early novels, *A Few Green Leaves* is equally pervaded by a sense of things ending. Yet still Pym does not allow her heroine to *change* in any radical way; just as Letty ends *Quartet in Autumn* on a dubiously hopeful note,

'Life still held infinite possibilities for change',[35] so Emma at the end of *A Few Green Leaves*, despite having learnt all we know she has learnt in the course of the novel about the fallible and hapless Tom, ends thus:

Emma was going to stay in the village herself. She could write a novel and even, as she was beginning to realize, embark on a love affair which need not necessarily be an unhappy one.[36]

The problem created by this tension between what she says and what she sees results in a failure of the ironic nerve. Having depicted life for her heroines in all its sad inadequacy, Pym appears to feel the need to end on an upbeat note. This has the unfortunate effect of undermining the admirable detachment Rossen rightly praises, of softening the truth. In only one novel does the irony remain firm; we are allowed to feel no sympathy for its egocentric heroine; there is no attempt at a happy ending. This is a novel Pym had much difficulty in getting published, and perhaps those reverses and consequent rewriting played their part as much as Pym's own unhappy love affair with a younger man in making *The Sweet Dove Died* so effective.

It is a bleak portrayal of a wealthy middle-aged, middle-class woman, confident – unusually so for a Pym heroine – about her looks, her clothes, her choice of decor and ability to cook and charm. Leonora is portrayed as a predator, willing to evict an old lady from her house in order to take over a young man's life. Leonora is typified by these inner thoughts, so different from Wilmet's or Emma's:

> It was more agreeable to reflect on how dreadful poor Meg had looked and to pity her unfortunate situation;[37]

> Leonora sat rather stiffly in the car, wondering why she had come. It was ominous, the bed not yet being made, as if she wasn't really expected. She needed to be very well looked after this weekend ...[38]

> One would hardly want to be like the people who fill the emptiness of their lives with an animal, Leonora thought, going back into the house.[39]

The most striking aspect of this novel, apart from the extremely effective characterisation of Leonora, is that it has quite a complicated plot and a clear storyline. The failure of *Quartet in Autumn* and *A Few Green Leaves* is that they bear too obviously the signs of Pym's well-known and well-attested technique: the use of anthropological observation of customs and behaviour together with a simplistic reliance on caricature rather than characterisation. These features, added to the sombre tone, deprive these novels of what is best in the earlier ones, a delighted and pointed wit. The story of Leonora and her humiliation at the hands of Ned is never allowed to become pathetic; thus the novel triumphs as an example of what Pym is best at: the presentation of a small group of characters in a recognisable setting, in a recognisable era, in such a way as to show how 'behaviour', a term Pym was herself fond of using in her notebooks, ultimately becomes a way of being when life is insupportable and when one has no moral refuge. Leonora has after all behaved despicably and exploitatively throughout the novel; how refreshing it is not to be persuaded, as we are so often by Brookner, to sympathise with her, but to see her, and all those other fairly shallow and unsympathetic characters, as they are, without any of that softening I referred to earlier.

Superficially it might appear that Brookner and Pym have little in common: the one being a writer of urban and *European* mores, the other an observer of peculiarly English scenes, whether in town or country. Yet if we take Brookner's *Hotel Du Lac* and Pym's *The Sweet Dove Died* as being each writer's most successful *and* most typical – in their use of setting, character, event etc – then we can see that they do have much in common. They both clearly also appeal to a similar *middle-class* readership. Their heroines, Edith and Leonora, are both financially independent, yet they are unhappy; a man is necessary to complete their sense of fully being. Both heroines interact with a disparate trio of men; neither finds comfort and pleasure in their relationships with other women, who are always sizing them up, estimating their power as rivals, critical of their appearance and smug in a sense (usually fatally flawed) of their own superiority. It is an interesting and significant point about both Brookner's and Pym's heroines that while they are always well educated and can quote from literature, especially poetry – usually to impress an audience – literature never provides a resource: being *found* reading a slim volume is the aim, not actually reading it for its own sake. This last point is significant because it points up the *self-consciousness* of especially Edith and Leonora. They are always tremulously self-conscious, never self-aware. This is what makes them victims; they need approval, male approval, a need which should render them all the more pathetic since the men portrayed in the two novels are a pretty poor lot. They are weak, exploitative, insensitive, vain, self-important. This is largely true of all the novels of both writers. *This* is what makes it so sad, so depressing, that Brookner and Pym seem unable ever to articulate the truth evident in their work: that women, their women, waste their emotions and their lives, and potentially rewarding relationships with other women in the pursuit of men. In this at least they are both the true heirs of Austen's legacy: nothing, absolutely nothing, is so important for a woman as the love of a man, any man. Reading their novels, peopled as they are by unfulfilled spinsters, dissatisfied wives – for Wilmet is as much a victim as any other Pym heroine – a woman might be forgiven for thinking that little had indeed changed since

1800, and as the would-be iconoclast Penelope is made to express it in *An Unsuitable Attachment*:

> 'I suppose a wife should consider her husband's work before her own happiness,' Penelope agreed, for like many modern young women she had the right old-fashioned ideas about men and their work.[40]

One can hear the echo, faint and fruitless, of Virginia Woolf's bitter complaint:

> Women have served all these centuries as looking-glasses possessing the magic power of reflecting the figure of man at twice its natural size.[41]

In 1869 J S Mill wrote:

> We may safely assert that the knowledge which men can acquire of women, even as they have been and are, without reference to what they might be, is wretchedly imperfect and superficial, and always will be so, until women themselves have told all that they have to tell.[42]

Had he been able to read Brookner and Pym, he would not have found the experience edifying.

Despite the fact that Brookner and Pym clearly belong to a genre quite different in its conventions from the Gothic, the genre to which du Maurier and Stewart owe so much, as do the Mills & Boon writers and Beauman, discussed in later chapters, it cannot be denied that even here we can see the influence of that strand of nineteenth-century literary tradition. The novels may *appear* to be comedies of manners, and to partake of the reality of this world, but in fact, and this is far truer of Brookner than it is of Pym, who has, as I observed earlier, the saving grace of irony, the lives of their female characters are limited and indeed diminished by a sense of hollowness – a hollowness which marks the lack of a man, a prince to release them from their humdrum lives into the apparent glamour of fulfilment. To write so much of the failure of the fairytale and its happy ending is to admit that the paradigm of the fairytale informs one's narrative.

Unlike Pym's earlier critics, it is not her attention to detail I would criticise, but the failure of nerve, entirely understandable in the circumstances, which prevents her later novels from achieving that brilliance of detachment and wit which so inform *The Sweet Dove Died*. Both Pym and Brookner are stylish in a way that subsequent writers I am to discuss can never be, notably the simple-sentence addicts of the Mills & Boon repertoire, and the italicisation and capitalisation of Collins and Conran, yet thematically they are not so far apart. Prince Charming is as much their heroines' desire as it is that of heroines of less demanding novels. Style, as I said in the Introduction, is not really my theme, or the issue. Recurring thematic patterns and stereotyping of gender roles are. Neither Brookner nor Pym is innocent of creating and therefore reinforcing stereotypical patterns of male/female gender roles and expectations. A change of genre, it seems, need not necessarily signify a change in authorial attitude, whether to narratological device or characterisation. We may read these two writers expecting, because of their evident erudition and, especially in the case of Pym, often perceptive portrayals of human behaviour and relationships, that they will also engage with more modernist theories of structure. We may also hope, since they experienced fulfilling independent lives *without* marriage, that they might give at least a nod in the direction of feminism. But no, to challenge patriarchy is no more their intention than it is that of Mary Stewart. Their comedies of manners are just as traditional in their portrayal of women whose lives are but cyphers until validated by some man's approval as anything by Stewart. Their Cinderellas never get the prince; their Janes are doomed to Rochester-free fates. That is the only difference between them.

3

Crime Does Pay: The Novels of Dorothy L Sayers and P D James

In this age, when masterpieces of excellence have been executed by pro-
fessional men, it must be evident that in the style of criticism applied
to them the public will look for something of a corresponding
improvement, practice and theory must advance ... People begin to see
that something more goes to the completion of a fine murder than two
blockheads to kill and be killed, a knife, a purpose, and a dark lane.
Design, gentlemen, grouping, light and shade, poetry, sentiment, are
now deemed indepensable to attempts of this nature.[1]

Were De Quincey alive to read the novels of Dorothy L Sayers and
P D James, he would, I think, have to admit that apart from being
'gentlemen', they had done everything he could have wished to
the depiction of murder as a 'fine art'.[2] Not for them the simple
puzzle outlined by Ernest Mandel in *Delightful Murder* (1984): 'The
problem, the Initial Solution, the Complication, the Period of
Confusion, the Dawning Light, the Solution, the Explanation'.[3]

Sayers and James add two major elements to the previously
simple detective story genre: the conventions of the fairy and
Gothic tale, and literary aspirations. For both of them, as for
Ngaio Marsh, Josephine Tey and Margery Allingham, it is not
enough that their hero should be a successful detective, he must
also be a Romantic hero. He, and it always is a he – heroines are
always ultimately subservient to him – is attractive to women,
sensitive, intelligent. Above all he must never look like a policeman.
And although James's, Tey's and Marsh's heroes *are* members of
the Force they are swiftly identified as superior mortals compared
with those the reader might actually meet. One of the ways in
which this superiority is achieved also attempts to fulfil that
other aspiration, towards literary respectability, which is such a
marked feature of especially Sayers and James. Their heroes write
poetry. Even in the middle of an investigation. Lord Peter Wimsey
completes a metaphysical sonnet partially written by Harriet
Vane, in *Gaudy Night*,[4] and Dalgleish, James's hero, pens this while
surrounded by mayhem on the Norfolk coast:

Remember me, you said, at Blythburgh,
As if you were not always in my mind
And there could be an art to bend more sure
A heart already wholly you inclined.
Of you, the you enchanted mind bereave
More clearly back your image to receive,
And in this unencumbered holy place
Recall again an unforgotten grace.
I you possessed must needs remember still
At Blythburgh my love, or where you will.[5]

Not only do they *write* poetry, they quote from literature; literary references abound, much in the manner that they do in Mary Stewart's novels (see Chapter 1), and for the same reason: to claim literary status for their texts. Both Sayers and James make extraordinary claims for their work. Whether these claims are valid is, in part, the argument of this chapter. That they both owe much to the fairy/Gothic tradition is my other contention.

If we consider the sources of the detective story genre the reasons for this particular legacy become clear. In their interesting and insightful book *Lust to Kill* (1986), Deborah Cameron and Elizabeth Fraser discuss and explain not only the continuing public appetite for so-called True Crime stories but also the concomitant development of the narrative which foregrounds the pursuer rather than the doer of these crimes. Their helpful hypothesis, that sympathy moved in the course of the nineteenth century from the criminal to the detective, and that that movement paralleled the change from the Gothic/Romantic hero to a central persona who more accurately reflected the moral concerns of the Victorian era, sheds light also on the development of the twentieth-century detective hero. Particularly as created by women.

Raymond Chandler criticised Sayers:

Her kind of detective story was an arid formula which could not even satisfy its own implications. It was second grade literature because it was not about the things that could make first grade literature. If it started out to be about real people ... they must very soon do unreal things in order to form the artificial pattern required by the plot. When they did unreal things, they ceased to be real themselves. They became cardboard lovers and papier-mache villains and detectives of exquisite and impossible gentility.[6]

Whether or not Chandler's own fiction achieved the level of 'first grade literature' is of course debatable. What is interesting is that he seems to think that Sayers aimed to do just that. Whoever is trying to achieve this would seem to be attempting the impossible, given the fact that this particular genre of literature is reducible to certain necessary elements (see Mandel, above). As John Cawelti says, it is essentially 'formulaic'.[7] P D James herself admits as much in her essay on Sayers: 'It has been said that the formula for a successful detective story is 50% good detection, 25% character and 25% what the writer knows best'.[8] And the *purpose* of 'formulaic' literature, according to Cawelti:

> is not to make me confront motives and experiences in myself that I might prefer to ignore but to take me out of myself by confirming an idealized self-image. Thus, the protagonists of formulaic literature are typically better or more fortunate in some ways than ourselves.[9]

Cawelti's point links usefully with Cameron and Fraser, cited earlier; like the romance, the detective novel partakes of the Gothic/Romantic. In other words it uses devices, formulae, shorthand, in order to encourage the reader to work out the puzzle, because that, ultimately is the detective writer's aim. It also, in its later manifestations, where the 'noble bandit'[10] has mutated into the evil criminal, endows its new hero, the detective, with not only the requisite moral stance of the late nineteenth, twentieth century, but also the superhuman powers once associated with the boundary-breaking, amoral Byronic hero. But as we shall see, both Sayers and James allowed their heroes to partake not only of the massive and imaginative intelligence of the archetypal detective hero, Sherlock Holmes, but also of the sexual irresistibility and aristocratic superiority of a Romantic hero. My contention is also that, as a result of this, the formulae, shorthand, in terms of characterisation and setting that they use, is unlike and serves a purpose quite other than that of Conan Doyle's use of the violin, cocaine and tobacco in a Persian slipper to identify his character swiftly to the reader.

With Sayers and James there is always something of a moral dilemma confronting the hero; he is engaged with more than the mere crime. He becomes more important than the crime. It is certain that one clue to the appeal not only of Sayers' novels, but also those of James, lies in what James calls : 'what the writer knows best'. James's background as a civil servant working in the field of forensic science supplies her (and her reader) with detail not available to (or perhaps desired by) other crime writers. Her display of sangfroid when detailing the most horrific of fatal injuries, as at the very beginning of *A Taste for Death* (1986) undoubtedly adds an air of verisimilitude to her narratives which the more discreet stories of an Agatha Christie could be said to lack:

> One corpse had slipped from the low single bed to the right of the door and lay staring up at her, the mouth open, the head almost cleft from the body. She saw again the severed vessels, sticking like corrugated pipes through the clotted blood.[11]

Similarly Sayers' display of often arcane knowledge, whilst undoubtedly irritating to some readers, nevertheless adds conviction to novels such as *Murder Must Advertise* (1933), which draws on her experience of working as a copywriter in an advertising agency, and *The Nine Tailors* (1934) (thought by many to be her best novel), where the twist is that the demonstration of her knowledge of bell-ringing conceals quite effectively from the reader the fact that it is the bells which commit the murder. 'What the writer knows best' can, however, equally prove her downfall; in *Gaudy Night* (1935) for example, she: '"deliberately set out to say things which, in a confused way, I had been wanting to say all my life" about the overwhelming importance of the integrity of the mind.'[12] And while, as James says, *Gaudy Night* 'has an attraction for lovers of Oxford',[13] it is, as James also says:

> not among her most successful detective novels, although it has an attraction ... for those *romantics* [my emphasis] primarily interested in the progress of the love affair between Peter Wimsey and Harriet Vane.[14]

In fact, of course, what has happened in *Have His Carcase* and *Gaudy Night* is that the ideal 25 per cent character has assumed a greater portion of the writer's interest, to the detriment of the supposed 50 per cent 'good detection' referred to by James. As James points out: 'by the time she wrote *Gaudy Night*, Miss Sayers, like her alter ego [Harriet Vane], has become dangerously enamoured of her aristocratic sleuth.'[15]

Most critics notably praise Sayers for her earlier Wimsey novels, specifically *Murder Must Advertise, Five Red Herrings* (1931) and *The Nine Tailors*, where one of the arts of the detective story writer, as pointed out by Cawelti (1976), of making us live out the explication and denouement of the crime along with the detective himself,[16] is most clearly demonstrated. As Wimsey discovers mystery after mystery, destroys alibi after alibi, we accompany him. Once Wimsey has fallen for Harriet Vane, as he does in *Strong Poison* (1930), it seems he is doomed to 'dwindle into a husband' (to rephrase Congreve). Although *Strong Poison* itself has all the elements of Sayers' particularly effective 'good detection' – the secret collection of nail parings and the necessary correcting of the police – once Harriet Vane is released from Holloway Prison, Wimsey and the books are never the same again. James gives us a clue as to what has happened when she cites Sayers' own *Introduction to Tales of Detection* (1936):

> no kind of fiction can survive for very long cut off from the great interests of humanity and from the mainstream of contemporary literature. We can now handle the mechanical elements of the plot with ease of long practice; we have yet to discover the best way of combining these with the serious artistic treatment of the psychological elements, so that the intellectual and the common man can find common ground for enjoyment in the mystery novel as they once did in Greek or Elizabethan tragedy.[17]

This quotation indicates precisely the point I made earlier concerning the literary aspirations of Sayers, Marsh and James. It indicates a tension between the relatively simple demands of the detective story and the ambitions of these writers to make something more, both of the story and, more importantly, of the hero figure. These ambitions manifest themselves textually, much as they do in Mary Stewart's novels, in the widespread use of quotation and literary reference.

Sayers' delineation of the Wimsey character, much in the manner of the Baroness Orczy, with her Sir Peter Blakeney as a most unlikely Scarlet Pimpernel, included a 'silly-ass' element, this being part of the way in which he could conceal his cleverness from villains. But unlike Sherlock Holmes, Hercule Poirot, or even Miss Marple, Wimsey, with his nervous debility stemming from World War One experiences,[18] never rejoices in his successes, especially as they then led to the execution of the murderer. He is never, in other words, simply the intellect in pursuit of a solution. He was never, I would argue, the simple detective of exquisite and impossible gentility of Chandler's stricture, cited earlier. Nor does he quite become a 'cardboard lover', although he comes close. What Chandler failed to notice was what kind of a *hero* Wimsey is, rather than what kind of detective.

It is my contention that unlike his contemporary detective heroes but like many subsequent or even consequent heroes, especially those created by women, Wimsey, who may initially have been merely the means whereby the plot is unfolded – 'a by-product of the narrative structure, and as such, a compositional rather than a psychological entity',[19] – does, as James suggests; 'change almost out of recognition as book succeeds book'.[20] He does not, however, become human; he becomes a hero in the Romantic sense of the word; he thus embodies, as a character, as much the stereotypical hero of romantic fiction as the stereotypical detective. The attraction of the Vane/Wimsey novels then is of the resultant tension between the commanding intellect of the detective in pursuit of wrongdoers – his usual role – and the abject passion of the unrequited lover.

That this is common to many women detective story writers is demonstrated in much the same situation being created in *Artists in Crime* (1938) and *Death in a White Tie* (1938) by Ngaio Marsh, when her aristocratic hero, now actually also a policeman, meets and falls in love with the painter Agatha Troy; indeed in *Artists in Crime* Troy is a possible suspect whom Alleyn has to interrogate. Alleyn (note the literary dramatic connotations of the name) also 'had a bad war' and is distressed by death, although this time of the victims rather than the convicted felons. Here it is Troy who finds execution unacceptable; nonetheless he wins her – an accurate description of his attitude – but only after the action of a second novel (note the use of language here; I have quoted at some length in order to give a taste of what is typical of the extent to which the lover-hero overwhelms the detective):

Alleyn pulled her hand down against his lips.
There was complete silence. Everything he had ever felt; every frisson, the most profound sorrow, the least annoyance, the greatest joy and the smallest pleasure had been but preparation for this moment when her hand melted against his lips. Presently he found himself leaning over her. He still held her hand like a talisman and he spoke against the palm.

'This must be right. I swear it must be right. I can't be feeling this alone. Troy?'

'Not now,' Troy whispered. 'No more, now. Please.'

'Yes'.

'Please.'

He stooped, took her face between his hands, and kissed her hard on the mouth. He felt her come to life beneath his lips. Then he let her go.

'And don't think I shall ask you to forgive me,' he said. 'You've no right to let this go by. You're too damn particular by half, my girl. I'm your man and you know it.'

They stared at each other.

'That's the stuff to give the troops,' Alleyn added.

'The arrogant male.'

'The arrogant turkey-cock,' said Troy shakily.[21]

If one did not know the context of this scene, just before the dénouement of a thriller, one would be forgiven for believing it to come from a woman's magazine or a Mills & Boon novel.

Marsh's hero, like Wimsey, is impossibly handsome, intelligent, aristocratic; these heroes' only weaknesses are entirely acceptable in terms of *romantic* rather than detective fiction. They dislike being the means whereby others get executed, and they fall madly and desperately and, for a flattering length of time unrequitedly, in love with independent and intelligent women: Vane is a detective novelist, Troy a painter; both are successful and financially independent.

Most of the other female characters in Sayers's and Marsh's novels are recognisable stereotypes; they appear in all the novels with depressing regularity. They are: tarts with or without hearts; middle-aged neurotic spinsters – even Sayers' resourceful Miss Climpson is not devoid of irritating female mannerisms (*vide* Lakoff[22]) such as writing in italics; or they are beautiful and silly – these can be young or middle-aged; or old and silly; these latter categories usually provide information/assistance in Sayers' novels, victim material/obstruction of the police in Marsh's. Stereotyping of female characters is not unexpected in any crime narrative; it is after all a genre in which (*pace* Sara Paretsky and other contemporary practitioners) males predominate in both criminal and detective roles. It may even be a necessary kind of 'shorthand' giving the writer more time to construct the important part of the story, the *plot*. However it is doubly depressing to see both Sayers and Marsh create potentially interesting female characters like Vane and Troy only to subvert their pretensions to cleverness, as Sayers does with Vane in *Gaudy Night*, or marginalise them as Marsh does with Troy. Alleyn, having met Troy in the course of a criminal investigation, is incapable of allowing her any part in his subsequent cases even when it is through her job, as an artist, that many of his cases come to light. (By 'part' I mean that she is considered too fragile even to discuss them.) Troy is packed off home in *A Clutch of Constables* (1968), to bed in countless others; usually on the pretext that her *art* must never be interfered with.

Sayers of course virtually abandoned Wimsey after his marriage to Vane in *Busman's Honeymoon*, but during their courtship the same masculine protectiveness emerges, not only obviously in *Strong Poison*, where Wimsey saves Vane from the gallows, but also in *Have His Carcase*, where he uses his influence to prevent the Press and the police from accusing her of yet another murder. As in *Strong Poison*, she resents his arrogant assumption of the saviour role, but by *Gaudy Night* Vane 'naturally' turns to him for help. *Gaudy Night* is an interesting novel in that, as her own words cited earlier show, it is the only one in which Sayers is at all overtly didactic. It is about the rights of women to equal educational provision, to claims of equal intellectual integrity. It elevates those rights above the supposed loyalties of a wife and mother; it would *seem* therefore to be a novel in which Vane is to be allowed to assert her independence. During most of the narrative Wimsey is in fact absent – on diplomatic work, saving the world from war. And Vane, as in *Have His Carcase*, is the focaliser by whom the narrative is mediated. The setting is an Oxford women's college and we might reasonably expect some departure from stereotypical characterisation. But in fact the same female stereotypes recur, even if this time thinly disguised by student/donnish gowns: the flirt, the embittered spinster, the beautiful and good, the beautiful and silly, the vulnerable middle aged and old.

The problem with the novel is that it is primarily concerned with Vane's gradual realisation, after five years of Wimsey's courtship, that she is in love with him. What it also shows, to the point of embarrassment, is how lovable he is. All the women dons fall for him, dressing up for his visit, commenting on his looks, berating Vane jealously for her behaviour with him; the criminal even breaks her antique chess set because she hasn't treated Wimsey properly! All events conspire to make the novel preeminently a paean of love, not just on Vane's part, but also on Sayers'. As James says, 'dangerously enamoured'.[22]

Sayers tells us how Wimsey admires Vane and encourages her to write and to be herself; what she *shows* us is Vane succumbing, in her own words:

> 'I have been facing one fact for some time,' said Harriet, staring out with unseeing eyes into the quad, 'and that is, that if I once gave way to Peter, I should go up like straw.'[24]

The 'crime' that Vane is supposed to be uncovering is not so very dreadful, yet she makes a terrible mess of it; almost fatally late she turns to Wimsey for help, and of course he solves the mystery instantly, and with the aid of another man, not Vane. It is depressing to see Vane crumble and break down, but above all it is depressing to see her *fail*. In *Strong Poison* and *Have His Carcase* she was, despite the odd lapse, admirably self-possessed, but in *Gaudy Night* she becomes the archetypal Sleeping Beauty, finally awakened by her truly handsome prince:

> Accepting rebuke, he relapsed into silence, while she studied his half-averted face. Considered generally, as a facade, it was by this time tolerably familiar to her, but now she saw details, magnified as it were by some glass in her own mind. The flat setting and fine scroll-work of the ear, and the height of the skull above it. The glitter of close-cropped hair where the neck-muscles lifted to meet the head. A minute sickle-shaped scar on the left temple. The faint laughter-lines at the corner of the eye and the droop of the lid at its outer end. The gleam of golden down on the cheekbone. The wide spring of the nostril. An almost imperceptible beading of sweat on the upper lip and a tiny muscle that twitched the sensitive corner of the mouth. The slight sun-reddening of the fair skin and its sudden whiteness below the base of the throat. The little hollow above the points of the collar-bone. He looked up; and she was instantly scarlet, as though she had been dipped in boiling water. Through the confusion of her darkened eyes and drumming ears some enormous bulk seemed to stoop over her. Then the mist cleared. His eyes were riveted upon the manuscript again, but he breathed as though he had been running.
>
> So, thought Harriet, it has happened. But it happened long ago. The only new thing that has happened is now I have got to admit it to myself. I have known it for some time. But does he know it? He has very little excuse, after this, for not knowing it. Apparently he refuses to see it, and that may be new ...[25]

It should not surprise us that the next moment he is buying her a necklace like a dog-collar, ostensibly to protect her from murderous attack, but actually, as revealed by his intention of having his name inscribed on it, to denote his triumphant possession of her. The consummation of Vane's and Wimsey's marriage in *Busman's Honeymoon* is given in every detail (for that time). Although the story involves the detection of yet another ingenious murderer, it is the apotheosis or nadir, depending on your view of the embarrassing profusion of verbose love scenes, of their fictive lives. Lord Peter appears again, somewhat bathetically,[26] duly paternal, and investigating the theft of some peaches. He has dwindled into a husband and father, and it would appear that Sayers, whose own experience of marriage and, separately, motherhood, was not happy, loses interest in him now he has fulfilled her dreams as well as Vane's.

One might expect that later writers would eschew so familiar a path, so littered as it is with echoes of Gothic/Romantic fiction. But no. Few other 'Queens of Crime' have followed Agatha Christie's example of choosing two unexpected and certainly anti-archetypal hero figures: an old spinster lady, Miss Jane Marple, and a narcissistic but asexual Belgian, Hercule Poirot. Margery Allingham chose an aristocrat for her detective hero; Albert Campion, someone so highly born that we are never told his real name and family. He too, like Wimsey, has a loyal and resourceful butler, and is infinitely cleverer than the Plods who appear in her stories. He, like Wimsey (in 1986), has recently appeared in a TV version of the stories, suggesting again their continuing appeal.

One might expect that at some point the real police would figure as the true detectives, and at first glance therefore the Inspector Roderick Alleyn of Ngaio Marsh's novels and Josephine Tey's Inspector Grant would appear to be about to redress the balance. But again no. Alleyn is the younger son of an earl. Grant has independent means. Like Lord Peter Wimsey and subsequently P D James's Adam Dalgliesh, they are tall and handsome with long lean fingers, they are sensitive and well-tailored; neither Alleyn nor Grant is ever guilty of *looking* like a policeman. They have the right of entry to the most upper-crust of suspects and they never age. Alleyn's sexual attractiveness to Marsh's stereotypical villainesses and victims continues unabated for 40 years! Although Alleyn rises in the ranks, his unfortunate subordinates, truly PC

Plods – Inspector Fox and the Scene of Crime men, Bailey and Thompson – never change. Marsh, perhaps, being a New Zealander, never knew how the English police force really works. Certainly she manifests in her novels a love of the aristocracy which amounts to a severe crush. Unlike Sayers, she never married, and this may explain the idyllic relationship which Troy and Alleyn enjoy, again for over 40 years. She does allow them to have a son, but once he is past early youth he disappears.

This love affair with an idealised policeman manifests itself just as clearly in P D James's much more recent novels featuring Adam Dalgliesh. This is despite her expressed intention of being a writer in a different mould from Sayers:

> She is, however, slightly impatient with the 'classical' detective novel of the kind that Agatha Christie or Dorothy L Sayers produced between the wars, which assumes that the world is a limited place where all things can be known, and which in consequence is bound to be orderly. Her novels are concerned not just with puzzle but with the corrosive aspects of crime: 'the moral basis is that murder is uniquely wrong'.[27]

Dalgliesh, like Wimsey and Alleyn is also a sensitive soul although in his case this is manifested in his being a poet. A published poet. Like Wimsey in *Gaudy Night* Dalgliesh has a turn for the metaphysical and we are given an example of his work in *Unnatural Causes*, quoted earlier in this chapter. James herself has considerable experience of the world of forensic science and her novels are certainly 'realistic' in their forensic detail, again see above, but in characterisation she, too, has Sayers' tendency to use stereotypical figures for her victims/villainesses and to endow her hero with superhuman powers. He is even more like the nineteenth-century Romantic hero from whom he clearly derives; his past is outlined to us in virtually every novel in which he plays a prominent role: he is the only child of an East Anglian vicar; his mother died young and he himself lost his wife and son in childbirth:

> Dalgliesh thought: I don't want to hear this. I don't want to listen to their pain. That was what the consultant obstetrician had said to him when he had gone to take a last look at his dead wife with her newborn son in the crook of her arm, both of them composed in the nothingness of death. A chance in a

million. As if there could be comfort, almost pride, in the knowledge that chance had singled out your family to demonstrate the arbitrary statistics of human fallibility.[28]

This tragedy endows him with particular sensitivity to young death, to the tragic nature of life. Small wonder that his superiors mistrust him:

> Nichols [Assistant Commissioner] was the senior in rank but this gave him small satisfaction when he knew that Dalgliesh could have outstripped him had he chosen. This lack of concern about promotion, which Dalgliesh never condescended to justify, he saw as a subtle criticism of his own more ambitious preoccupations. He deplored the poetry, not on principle, but because it had conferred prestige and, therefore, couldn't be regarded as a harmless hobby like fishing, gardening or woodwork. A policeman, in his view, should be satisfied with policing. An added grievance was that Dalgliesh chose most of his friends from outside the force and those fellow officers he consorted with weren't always of an appropriate rank. In a junior officer that would have been regarded as a dangerous idiosyncrasy and in a senior it had a taint of disloyalty. And to compound these delinquencies, he dressed too well.[29]

That the poetry plays an important part in James's concept of Dalgliesh's character seems to be borne out by the number of times it is referred to, 16 times at least in *A Taste for Death*, when Dalgliesh's fear that he may never write another poem becomes a kind of subplot parallel to the murder plot. This acquaintance with literature also has the effect of making his subordinates feel inferior, Dalgliesh being perceived by them as superiorly sensitive and imaginative. As in the case of Alleyn, and again over a considerable period of time – from *Cover her Face* (1962) to *Devices and Desires* (1989) Dalgliesh has, despite promotion, never aged and remains dauntingly attractive to the women he has to interrogate. Almost as if following the Sayers/Marsh pattern, he meets an early mistress, Deborah Riscoe, in the course of an investigation; he finds her mother guilty of murder. Naturally this dampens their relationship but it develops in subsequent texts and only ends with her departure to America in *Unnatural Causes*. (It is she to whom the poem quoted earlier is addressed.) James is herself perhaps too enamoured of him to allow any relationship of a permanent nature to detract from his continuing air of world-weariness and detachment.

James appears to prefer Dalgliesh to be aloof and self-aware. He lives in a flat in Queenhythe overlooking the Thames – an early Docklands yuppie? – and likes fast cars. His status as a grieving widower, however far in the past the bereavement is, remains a constant in our minds, and allows James to present him as a proficient but cold lover, a man afraid of another potentially painful commitment. James thus achieves at once the suffering Romantic hero with the (scarcely-concealed) secret in his past, and the cold-hearted lover of the James Bond era. In another way too she manages to have her cake and eat it; although Dalgliesh is a serving officer, and must therefore obey the etiquette of the force – he cannot simply assume command of inadequate rural Plods in the manner of a Wimsey – James often places him on vacation at the scene of a crime: *Unnatural Causes*, *The Black Tower*, *Devices and Desires*. Thus he can operate in the accepted *deus ex machina* manner and unravel the truth unhampered by report filling or the questions of inferior or superior officers.

As far as her other characters are concerned James, like Sayers, does her own sex few favours. Both of them use the stock stereotypes of romantic fiction for their general (that is, not heroic or central) female characters; they are all maidens, whores, mothers or witches. James particularly seems to delight in depressingly detailed descriptions of the peculiar uglinesses of women; witness this description of Sylvia Kedge in *Unnatural Causes*:

> The girl would have been called unusual, perhaps even beautiful, if only one could have forgotten those twisted ugly legs, braced into calipers, the heavy shoulders, the masculine hands distorted by her crutches. Her face was long, brown as a gypsy's and framed by shoulder length black hair brushed straight from a centre parting. It was a face which could have held strength and character but she had imposed on it a look of piteous humility.[30]

Or this of Evelyn Matlock in *A Taste for Death*:

> She was, he guessed, in her late thirties, and was uncompromisingly plain in a way it struck him few women nowadays were. A small sharp nose was imbedded between pudgy cheeks on which the threads of broken veins were emphasised rather than disguised by a thin crust of make-up. She had a primly censorious mouth above a slightly receding chin already showing

the first slackness of a dewlap. Her hair, which looked as if it had been inexpertly permed, was pulled back at the sides but frizzed over the high forehead in the poodle-like fashion of an Edwardian[31]

She has very little sympathy for the unfortunate and seems to be positively averse to social workers: see *A Taste for Death passim*. The men in her novels, even the villains, are the true objects of interest, being portrayed as having greater psychological depth than any of the women. In *Devices and Desires* the more beautiful the women, the more likely they are to be misguided and the more horrific their deaths – the intensely attractive Amy for example, who meets her death, in a most unlikely subplot, as a result of a lesbian relationship. One cannot help but feel a heavily moralistic hand here; she was not satisfied with single motherhood and the adoration of one male character, not to mention the passion of another, she turned to women, and this is how she looks when her corpse is found:

> On the Monday morning a retired tax officer, exercising his Dalmatian dog on the beach, saw the animal sniffing round what looked like a white slab of lard entwined with seaweed, rolling and gliding at the edge of the tide. As he drew close the object was sucked back by the receding wave then taken up by the next surge and flung at his feet and he found himself gazing in incredulous horror at the torso of a woman neatly severed at the waist. For a second he stood petrified, staring down as the tide boiled in the empty sockets of the left eye and swayed the flattened breasts.[32]

In this novel James brings us up to date. This time the familiar East Anglian coastline is dominated by a nuclear power station. Despite a subplot which is at best tenuous, and at worst incredible, the plot-patterns, and characterisation and relationships remain very similar to those in the much earlier *Cover her Face*; again the unmarried mother comes to a bad end; most marriages are unhappy; most of the women are unfulfilled, demanding and bitter. And of course the local police are no match for the superior perceptions of Dalgliesh. This novel is particularly disappointing in its actual reversion to type, beneath the trappings of a more up-to-date society, since there do appear to be real attempts at modernisation in the preceding *A Taste for Death*.

In Inspector Kate Miskin Dalgliesh has at last a female subordinate, and one who is psychologically realised in some depth. However, like her fellow officer on the case, John Massingham – a reversion to detective fiction type with a vengeance, he is an earl's son – she is totally in awe of Dalgliesh and spends as much time in the novel thinking about how she may impress him as how she may solve the crime and sort out her family problems. And James in a curious passage details what Dalgliesh thinks is Massingham's attitude towards her, curious because it echoes much contemporary police thinking, and because Dalgiesh does not reject it:

> He would work with Kate Miskin loyally and conscientiously because he respected her as a detective and that was what he was required to do. But Dalgliesh knew that Massingham still half-regretted the days when women police-officers were content to find lost children, search female prisoners, reform prostitutes, comfort the bereaved and, if they hankered for the excitement of criminal investigation, were suitably occupied coping with the peccadilloes of juvenile delinquents. And, as Dalgliesh had heard him argue, for all their demands for equality of status and opportunity, putting them in the front line behind the riot shields, taking the petrol bombs, the hurled stones and now the bullets, only made the job of their male colleagues even more onerous. In Massingham's view the instinct to protect a woman in moments of high danger was deep-seated and ineradicable, and the world would be a worse place if it wasn't. He had, as Dalgliesh knew, grudgingly respected Kate's ability to look down at the butchered bodies in St Matthew's vestry and not be sick, but he hadn't liked her the better for it.[33]

Kate, despite being a policewoman, is actually a rewrite or reworking of an earlier James venture: the female detective heroine. Like Sayers, James has a Harriet Vane; Cordelia Gray appears in the unsubtly-titled *An Unsuitable Job for a Woman* (1972) and is also the heroine of *The Skull Beneath the Skin* (1982). Like Miskin she is, usefully and in the manner of romantic fiction, an orphan, a self-made woman, to all outward appearances a thoroughly emancipated post-60s woman. But this *appearance* is deceptive. All her craft is learned by Cordelia from her late partner, a failed detective who modelled himself on his idol, one Adam Dalgliesh. Despite her apparent defeat of Dalgliesh in *An Unsuitable Job for a Woman*, with the collusion of the redoubtable Miss Leaming, who, awaiting the arrival of the police says, 'What is there to be

frightened of? We shall be dealing only with men.'[34] Cordelia is
by no means the independent woman one might hope. When
involved in her investigation she feels alone and unhappy:

> Cordelia was suddenly oppressed with loneliness and
> melancholy. If Bernie were alive they would be discussing the
> case, cosily ensconced in the furthest corner of some Cambridge
> pub, insulated by noise and smoke and anonymity from the
> curiosity of their neighbours; talking low voiced in their own
> particular jargon.[35]

Dalgliesh, on the other hand, always enjoys his own company,
driving himself very fast, à la Wimsey, visiting old country
churches or bird sanctuaries alone, and returning contentedly to
his empty flat. In *The Skull Beneath the Skin* James takes Cordelia
to what is very much Ngaio Marsh territory and seems oddly dated
for a 1982 novel. It concerns a group of people gathered together
to put on a performance of *The Duchess of Malfi* on an island off
the Dorset coast. Dalgliesh does not appear in person in this
novel, although there is an intriguing reference to him:

> She guarded her privacy [like Dalgliesh himself and Kate Miskin,
> see below]. None of her friends and no one from the Agency
> had ever been in the flat. Adventures occurred elsewhere. She
> knew that if any man shared that narrow bed for her it would
> mean commitment. There was only one man she ever pictured
> there and he was a Commander of New Scotland Yard. She knew
> that he, too, lived in the City; they shared the same river. But
> she told herself that the brief madness was over, that at a time
> of stress and frightening insecurity [the action of *An Unsuitable
> Job for a Woman*] she had only been seeking for her lost father-
> figure. There was this to be said for a smattering of amateur
> psychology: it enabled one to exorcise memories which might
> otherwise be embarrassing.[36]

And of course it is necessary for his male power to validate
Cordelia's *bona fides* later in the narrative:

> 'The name Commander Adam Dalgliesh mean anything to
> you, Sergeant?'
>   There was no need to ask of what force. Only the Met had
> Commanders. Buckley said:

'I've heard of him, sir.'

'Who hasn't? The Commissioner's blue-eyed boy, darling of the establishment. When the Met, or the Home Office come to that, want to show that the police know how to hold their forks and what bottle to order with the canard a l'orange and how to talk to a Minister on level terms with his Permanent Secretary, they wheel out Dalgliesh. If he didn't exist, the Force would have to invent him.'

The gibes might be unoriginal but there was nothing second-hand about the dislike ...

'He could have had his own force by now – probably be chairing A.C.P.O. – if he hadn't wanted to stick to detection. That and personal conceit. The rest of you can struggle in the muck for the prizes ... He knows the girl, Cordelia Gray. They tangled together in a previous case ... No details offered and none asked for. But he's given her and that Agency a clean bill. Like him or not, he's a good copper, one of the best. If he says that Gray isn't a murderess I'm prepared to take that as evidence of a sort.'[37]

It goes without saying that Chief Inspector Grogan does *not* inspire the emotions in Cordelia that keep her hanging around the fringes of Dalgliesh's life. Poor Cordelia ominously appears in *his* stories, bringing flowers to *his* hospital bedside in *The Black Tower* (1975) and being apparently a frequent dining-partner in *A Taste for Death*:

> 'Incongruous people dining together. Adam Dalgliesh, poet-detective, with Cordelia Gray at Mon Plaisir, for example.'
>
> 'Your readers [said Dalgliesh] must lead very dull lives if they can find vicarious excitement in a young woman and myself virtuously eating duck à l'orange.'
>
> 'A beautiful young woman dining with a man over twenty years her senior is always interesting to our readers. It gives them hope. And you're looking very well, Adam.'[38]

In fact, if Cordelia Gray was in her early 20s in *An Unsuitable Job for a Woman*, she cannot be a young woman in *A Taste for Death*, and as for what age that makes Dalgliesh ...! Now of course, one might say that each novel exists in its own right; that Dalgliesh is recreated each time, and possibly anyway for a new readership. But in that case why does James reintroduce characters? Is it, as in Barbara Pym, out of mischief? Or is it that in fact she wants a sense of continuity in her novels? James's novels have become longer, often have more than one subplot, and include disquisitions on the state of society. The publication of *The Children of Men* (1992), her only non-detective novel and much concerned with religion, not to mention her elevation to the House of Lords, would seem to indicate that, as she hinted in the *Sunday Correspondent* interview quoted earlier, she wishes to be regarded as more than a mere writer of detective fiction.

There is no doubt that James's novels have acquired the context of the contemporary world; she is *au fait* with nuclear disarmers, as in *Devices and Desires*, and the necessary jargon associated with the problems of the inner-city poor – for whom she feels little sympathy, see *A Taste for Death*, but she is not really reconstructed. Women are only allowed limited and stereotypical roles in her novels. Even Cordelia Gray, resourceful and courageous though she is shown to be in both the novels in which she has a central part, ultimately falls under Dalgliesh's spell and becomes a marginal figure; James's experiment with a heroine for our more equal times is soon abandoned. And Kate Miskin, a more contemporary figure than Cordelia, being illegitimate and working class and having a tiresome old granny who lives in a council tower block, did not reappear in *Devices and Desires*, and may be yet another abandoned prototype. In any case her devotion to Dalgliesh, as man and boss, is so complete that in her thinking she often seems like his clone:

> The flat was her private world kept inviolate from colleagues in the police. Only her lover was admitted, and when Alan had first stepped through the door, uncurious, unthreatening, carrying as always his plastic bag of books, even his gentle presence had seemed for a moment a dangerous intrusion.[39]

However, her flat, unlike Dalgliesh's *is* violated, first by the inevitable arrival of her ailing grandmother, then by the murderer Kate has been pursuing, then by death and its attendants, the police. Like Cordelia Kate becomes a victim. Dalgliesh, on the other hand, only once becomes a victim, and that in the fairly atypical *The Black Tower*. This is atypical because it focuses much more centrally on Dalgliesh as a man rather than as a detective. It introduces him in a kind of victim role, in hospital, recovering from what was thought to be a fatal illness. The action of the narrative takes place during his convalescence and also during an apparent mid life crisis in the course of which he contemplates giving up the police. He becomes a victim, in the manner of Kate and Cordelia, in that the villain, for once, gets the upper hand and almost kills him.

For James, as for Sayers and Marsh and Tey, the detective is not only the hero, but the Hero, a figure owing as much to romantic as to detective fiction. And however potentially interesting, intelligent and independent any woman may seem, in the end she is relegated to that familiar role, of serving, in Woolf's words, cited earlier: 'all these centuries as looking-glasses possessing the magic and delicious power of reflecting the figure of man at twice its natural size.'[40]

It is a sad fact that to find detectives who seem to be fallible human beings with everyday marriages and commonplace activities like filling in reports we have to turn to male writers, especially such as Nicholas Freeling who has not only created two likeable but imperfect detective heroes, Van der Valk and Castang, but in their wives, Arlette and Vera, something approximating to credible female characters. Freeling shows that it is possible to use *ordinary* people in his novels; more recent English female writers of detective fiction, like Joan Smith, have tried to suggest more autonomous women, not entirely convincingly. And still Sayers, Marsh and Tey are being reprinted. James regularly tops the bestseller lists. Readers, and, according to Cameron and Fraser these are likely to be middle-aged women, still prefer that strangely romantic mysterious entity, the hero detective, and the more aristocratic and superiorly intellectual and imaginative he is the better.

4

Two for the Price of One:
The Novels of Mills & Boon

Real literature, like real art, reflects society as through the 'broken mirror' of the author's subjectivity, to repeat a formula of Trotsky's reiterated by Terry Eagleton. In Trivialliteratur *that subjectivity is absent, and society is 'reflected' only in order to cater, for commercial purposes, to some supposed needs of the readers.*[1]

Although Mandel is here referring to crime fiction, his critical observations would seem to apply far more forcefully to the novels published in this country by Mills & Boon, in the US by Harlequin and Silhouette. Though some serious critical attention has been paid to the American phenomenon, very little has actually been written on Mills & Boon as such.

Despite the efforts of Radway and Modleski, among others, to ascribe greater virtue to these texts than would strike any casual reader, there is no doubt that they are produced 'for commercial purposes'. As Margolies points out:

Unlike the traditional image of publishing which assumes the unique value of each book, Mills & Boon romance is presented as a commodity like tea or soap powder. Whereas literary publishers may advertise a new novel stressing the qualities that distinguish it from others, Mills & Boon advertise a general product, 'the rose of romance'. The product is sold in an easily recognizable package assuring the purchaser of standard quantity (192 pages of romance) and consistent quality.[2]

And no one can deny the marketing energy that has *pushed* its product, during the period I have been researching this topic, 1990–93, via free copies accompanying soap powder, a programme all to itself on BBC2[3], not to mention the hard sell, soft image purveyed in actual copies:

TAKE FOUR
BEST SELLER
ROMANCES
FREE!

> Best Sellers are for
> the true romantic!
> These stories are our
> favourite Romance
> titles re-published by
> popular demand.
>
> POST TODAY
> and we'll send you this
> cuddly Teddy Bear.
>
> PLUS a free
> mystery gift!
> we all love mysteries, and
> so we've an intriguing gift
> especially for you.

This advertisement appears in the text[4] of *The Alpha Man* (1992), a Euromance by Kay Thorpe. On the front of *Leader of the Pack* (1991), by Catherine George, appear the words:

> FREE HOLIDAY SPENDING MONEY
> and a chance to win
> a luxury holiday.

Many covers encourage readers to subscribe to a mail order service, which supplies four new titles each month before they appear in the shops. Additionally, readers can select the *kind* of romance they wish to read; the Euromance is a new departure, apparently intending to reflect our 1992 entry into the wider European market. As we shall see, European man is *not* an improvement on Anglo-Saxon man. Other readers may select Medical Romances, like *Doctor on Skye* (1992), by Margaret O'Neill, in which the usual love story is leavened with tasty discussions of fungoid infections and the nature of undines. Under the Masquerade imprint Mills & Boon publishes Historical Romances, which obviously partake of some of the usual elements of the Gothic tale, but are in fact the recipe as before simply removed to another time and place. Silhouette, publishing in the UK, offers a series called *Desire*, supposedly rather hotter stuff than the Romances; they too advertise a mail order service *and* the cuddly toy.

In her interesting essay on Harlequin and Silhouette novels, Janice Radway seems at pains to deny their formulaic nature. She argues that critics have derogated these texts because 'they focus only on the texts in isolation'.[5] She grounds her essay, and a subsequent book, in analysis of reader-response. Thus she claims that the women in her research sample read the novels for escape, as is generally agreed, but escape of a very specific kind. While reading the novels her readers cut themselves off from their duties as wives and mothers and in entering the world of the text rediscovered their own lost experience of being mothered, that is, cared for protectively. She argues further that the women in her sample are very selective about the kinds of romance they like – that they dislike excessively brutal men and wimpish heroines, and that they are not too keen on too much sex.

This *use* of Harlequins (both Radway and Modleski are writing in an American context) is also adduced by Tania Modleski in *Loving with a Vengeance: Mass-Produced Fantasies for Women* (1982), as a sign that women manipulate texts for their own purposes, that as *active* readers they are therefore not accepting of the patriarchal ideology seemingly embedded in the texts. In an interesting but very debatable passage Modleski says:

> A great deal of our [sic] satisfaction in reading these novels comes, I am convinced, from the elements of a revenge fantasy, from our conviction that the woman is bringing the man to his knees and that all the while he is being so hateful, he is internally grovelling, grovelling, grovelling.[6]

This would seem to be of a piece with the 'taming' by maiming that Jane Eyre achieves in her relationship with Rochester. Modleski's comments continue with what further seems to be an echo of the Cathy/Heathcliff relationship in *Wuthering Heights*:

> In most of the novels, the hero finally becomes aware of the heroine's 'infinite preciousness' after she has run away, disappeared, fallen into a raging river, or otherwise shown by the threat of her annihilation how important her life is.[7]

Modleski agrees that this is a 'childish fantasy',[8] but argues that it explains the amount of anger felt against the hero by the heroine in the course of the story. When all else fails, 'he'll be sorry when I'm dead'. Of course the difference is that Cathy *does* die, and only half-way through the novel, and that Heathcliff far from being 'sorry' is enraged and seeks vengeance through Cathy's child for her perceived abandonment of him. The problem is that both Brontë novels operate on the level of what Modleski herself calls 'high art';[9] to put it at its simplest there is much more going on at the subtextual level in them than would ever be permitted in a Harlequin/Mills & Boon text.

As I said in the Introduction, it seems clear that all the critics who have handled, and I use that word advisedly, the Harlequin phenomenon, have handled it as if it were a hot coal, or an object of great fragility. They seem unwilling to deal with it as they might with a novel by any of the other writers I have discussed up to now. It as if it were surrounded by a kind of barrier labelled 'popular culture' and therefore lies outside the conventional literary critical field. Why, I wonder, does one find essays on it among studies of TV soaps and series? It is accorded the same degree of seriousness, and is, I would hazard, subject to the same troubling awareness of political correctness. In other words criticism of the texts might seem like criticism of the readership. No one appears to feel anything like this angst when criticising science fiction/fantasy, thrillers or detective stories, especially those written by men.

Radway, Modleski and Margolies are all anxious not to appear to condescend to the novels they are discussing; Margolies even makes a point of saying that the novels he analysed were not all equally bad! Some indeed come in for praise because of their offering of positive role models.[10] However praiseworthy this attitude may be, it cannot conceal certain undeniable facts about the novels. First, the novels are not only formulaic in structure, they are *written* to a formula. As Margolies admits:

> Awareness of the audience's taste controls much of the writing. In effect, there is editorial direction, not in positively demanding certain production, but in refusing severely non-conforming work, a form of censorship called 'giving the readers what they want' but guided by commercial rather than ideological principles.[11]

> the company which produces them [Harlequin Romances] requires its writers to follow a strict set of rules and even dictates the point of view from which the narrative must be told.[12]

In the 1993 BBC2 programme 'celebrating' the Mills & Boon romance, subtitled *A Guide to Writing Romantic Fiction*, the presenter,

Susie Blake, insisted that she could not tell people how to write successful romantic fiction, yet the programme consisted of discussions among authors concerning ideal plot structures and characters, editorial meetings between authors and editors, and analyses of particularly successful recipes. The essential recipe is cited in Modleski:

> Harlequins are well-plotted, strong romances with a happy ending. They are told from the heroine's point of view and in the third person. There may be elements of mystery or adventure but these must be subordinate to the romance. The books are contemporary and settings can be anywhere in the world as long as they are authentic. [13]

The second point on which Radway, Modleski and Margolies are agreed is that women read these novels to escape. Modleski's chapter on Harlequins is actually entitled *The Disappearing Act*. She claims that whilst women are reading they disappear from the real world, which makes so many demands on them, into the world of the text. However, dependent as her discussion is on psychoanalytic theory, she goes further than Radway allows in suggesting that this disappearing act results in feelings of guilt on the part of the woman, who can assuage these feelings only by reading yet another text; in this way Modleski explains her categorisation of Harlequins as 'hysteric' texts:

> a process which 'leads further and further away from the self becoming the basis for gratification and experience into a sense of emptiness, experiential deficiency and a wish to regress back into the dependency of early childhood as a haven'. [14]

Modleski carefully does not relegate the Harlequin to the status of a box of chocolates but, as we shall see in her conclusion, seems very confused as to exactly what she thinks of it.

Radway is determined to reject Modleski's reading, yet as I mentioned earlier, her research sample would seem to support it:

> When asked why they read romances, the Smithton women overwhelmingly cite escape or relaxation as their goal. They use the word 'escape', however, both literally and figuratively. On the one hand, they value their romances highly because the act of reading them literally draws the women away from their present surroundings. Because they must produce the meaning

of the story by attending closely to the words on the page, they find that their attention is withdrawn from concerns that plague them in reality.[15]

I should point out that 'producing the meaning of the story' indicates the focus of Radway's essay: the women are interacting with the text, *not* merely being manipulated by it. As I said in the Introduction and hope to show in this chapter, I think this distinction is a tenuous one.

Margolies' description of the nature of the 'escape' enjoyed by the reader would seem closer to the truth, and would seem also to take him dangerously near the edge he seems so eager to avoid – that of actually criticising the texts:

> The reader is not required to accommodate herself to the objectivity or rationality of plot, the looking outward, the integration of self in world; rather, she is encouraged to sink into feeling – and to feel without regard for the structure of the situation or circumstances that give rise to it. This, I suppose, is why she reads Mills & Boon rather than a thriller.[16]

Or even, one might add, why she reads Mills & Boon rather than a Gothic romance, since they do have quite complicated plots. Here, from Margolies, we have the definition of the Mills & Boon novel as warm bath. Warm bath, box of chocolates, cuddly toy, these all suggest women in search of comfort rather than the effortful reader supposed by Radway. A further point made by all three critics about the reader emphasises her essential passivity:

> Passivity, it seems, is at the heart of the romance-reading experience in the sense that the final goal of the most valued romances is the creation of perfect union in which the ideal male, who is masculine and strong, yet nurturant, finally admits his recognition of the intrinsic worth of the heroine. Thereafter, she is required to do nothing more than exist as the center of this paragon's attention. Romantic escape is a temporary but literal denial of the demands these women recognize as an integral part of their roles as nurturing wives and mothers. But it is also a figurative journey to a utopian state of total receptiveness in which the reader, as a consequence of her identification with the heroine, feels herself the passive *object* of someone else's attention and solicitude. The romance reader in effect is permitted the experience of feeling cared for, the

sense of having been affectively reconstituted, even if both are lived only vicariously.[17]

Modleski similarly shares Radway's positive reading of passivity, ending her chapter on Harlequins with this encomium of their effects:

> And if, on the one hand, the novels actually contribute to women's problems, on the other hand, a study of the romances shows cause for optimism. It is no mean feat for a grown woman to make herself disappear. As Freud frequently noted, an enormous amount of psychic energy is expended when an individual strives to attain a passive state. The reader of romances, contrary to the arguments of many popular literature critics, is engaged in an intensely active psychological process. The energy women now use to belittle and defeat themselves can be rechannelled into efforts to grow and explore ways of affirming and asserting the self. Moreover, the very fact that the novels must go to such extremes to neutralize women's anger and to make masculine hostility bearable testifies to the depths of women's discontent. Each novel, as we saw, is as much a protest against as an endorsement of the feminine condition. Finally, not all the female longings and desires expressed in Harlequins are regressive. Indeed, many of the contradictions I have discussed in this chapter derive from the attempt to adapt what for women are utopian ideals to existing circumstances. The desire to perform a disappearing act suggests women's suppressed wish to stop being seen in the old ways and to begin looking at their lives in ways that are perhaps yet to be envisioned.[18]

I have quoted this conclusion at such length because it reflects the actually unresolved contradictions at the centre of both Radway's and Modleski's critiques. They neither of them wish to derogate the texts for fear of seeming to derogate the romance readership; both therefore ascribe psychological benefits such as escape from the pressures of the real world, a sense of pleasurable abandonment, equally susceptible of achievement as I have indicated earlier, through the media of a warm bath, a box of chocolates, or a cuddly toy, to the reading of romance. Additionally both declare the reader to be an *active* user of the romance rather than its victim. You cannot, I would argue, both passively lie back and enjoy an escapist novel, and be aware of its raising your consciousness in some worthy feminist manner. Margolies is much closer to the truth in his discussion of the effects of romance reading:

> Once the conventions of the form become familiar to her, the romance reader knows she must understand the world through the eyes and feelings of the heroine. She wishes to enter the world of the heroine, the story, but there is only one door in, and she must assume a particular posture to go through it (usually passive subordination). If she finds the door too narrow or disconcertingly large – i.e. , if the ideology of any romance conflicts with her pleasure – she can read a different one (Mills & Boon's market research has shown romance readers to have clear and often limited taste); but if she assumes the posture often enough, it must begin to seem natural ...
>
> Fantasy, which might be thought to liberate through reorganizing the elements of reality in a more satisfying way, is in the Mills & Boon romance usually only an imaginative projection of confining forms of reality.[19]

Margolies' final point is I think most perceptive of the actual failure of Mills & Boon romances to provide a true fantasy experience, in the sense of encouraging the reader to perceive reality in an altered and enhanced way. As I said in the Introduction true fairy and folktales, unaffected by nineteenth-century moralising, can be illuminating. But unlike genuine fairy or folktales they do not show how life may be experienced as a learning experience, because, in their structure, style and characterisation they are endlessly repetitive, and more importantly, untrue to psychological reality. As Susie Orbach said, in a 1993 *Guardian* article:

> Romance is neither good nor bad per se. It has invested in it and projected on to it a variety of emotional needs. For lots of us, romance or the romantic phase of a relationship precedes the more humdrum workaday intimacies that are achieved in on-going committed relationships. The memories of that delicious early contact; the engrossing interest in another coupled to interest in oneself; the pleasure of erotic interchange; the capacity to experience love and to give it; all these aspects of romance underpin many people's attachments. Romance provides us with an emotional memory of what was possible and that remembrance can help weather the misunderstandings and difficult times in a relationship. We recall the energy

once felt and hope again to renew ourselves and our love through it.

But romance often doesn't turn into love ... Romance becomes the experience ...

For people trapped in the need to reiterate the high, romance becomes a drug with the search for it driven by the need for recompense. Romance feeds a starved heart.[20]

Orbach is writing about the need for romance itself, but what she says is true for the Mills & Boon romance; it too can become a drug. Mills & Boon clearly recognises this, in its repeated offer within the texts themselves of more and more examples promised for the cost of a stamp.

What then are Mills & Boon offering? Radway condemns literary critics for their rejection of the form on the basis of a single text; reading many has not improved my opinion of them. Rather the reverse. The repetition of plot, style and character seems deliberately to limit the reader's imagination. And nothing else is left to the imagination either. Joanna Russ in her essay on the Gothic romance[21] mocks their authors' insistence on detail; no Gothic heroine just dresses; she puts on a specific dress, jewellery and shoes, *and* matching handbag; she carefully makes up her face and does her hair. The rooms she moves in are described like features out of *Homes and Gardens*, and the meals she eats, even in the midst of the most suspenseful plot, are detailed enough for the reader to be able to recreate them, should she wish. Mary Stewart is particularly and disconcertingly guilty of this. After all if you think you are being pursued by a murderer would you have the time as Charity does, in *Madam Will You Talk?*, to appreciate an omelette aux fines herbes?[22]

One might argue that there is more justification for all this detail in a straight romance since the plot, true to the guidelines cited above, is entirely concerned with the development of the love affair between the main protagonists. Details of rooms, clothes and food take up time; they add to our knowledge of the tastes (and usually wealth) of the protagonists. What they also do, over and over again, is to insist on the superiority of these protagonists over mere mortals who exist in a real world. Not one of the heroes and heroines in the texts I have read is anything but extravagantly beautiful and desirable; no place here for the size 16 lady or the chap with the receding hairline and incipient paunch. One of these *does* appear in *Yesterday's Echoes* (1993), by Penny Jordan, but wouldn't you know it, he's the beast who raped our heroine when she was only 16. According to the BBC2 programme mentioned earlier, Mills & Boon is very aware of the changing role of women, and changed attitudes to sex, and feels it reflects these in its romances. Here are two descriptions of heroes From the May 1993 output:

> Dominic Savage was more handsome in maturity than when she had met him. Then she had thought him the most handsome boy she had ever seen, so compellingly attractive that she could hardly stop looking at him; eyes so blue, face just the right mixture of perfect features and strong masculinity, and the intriguing dimple at the base of his chin to break the rather uncompromising power of his square chin.[23]

> My God, she had forgotten how big Kieran Sinclair was!
> His profile was a beautiful but forbidding line. Fire sizzled across Tegan's nerve-ends as she registered the high forehead, a slashing straight nose that gave him the air of haughty arrogance he had used to intimidate Alana, a wide uncompromising but beautifully chiselled mouth, and a chin and jawline that indicated he was not in the habit of making compromises.[24]

Masculine power and inability to compromise, in addition to their sexual attractiveness, is what primarily denotes Mills & Boon heroes. No New Man here. When Tegan's (female) partner is held hostage in an Arab country, her husband is such a 'wimp' (a term used by Tegan, Tegan's Mother and of course the bold Kieran) that he is depressed and distraught. Kieran however casually goes off and rescues her, with the aid of some friendly banditti. Even when the hero is temporarily disadvantaged, as Professor James Macdonald is, by his blindness and leg ulcer, acquired as a result of a grenade in Sri Lanka, he is still dominant, and of course devastatingly handsome:

> The Professor's handsome face, half concealed though it was by the dark glasses covering both eyes, betrayed continuing anger. His lips were tightly compressed, nostrils of a splendid high-bridged nose flaring and a determined chin jutting mutinously ... He ran a thin brown hand through his mop of wiry hair, jet-black except where a snow-white streak lacerated it from temple to nape.[25]

Swap the Sri Lankan hand grenade for the fire at Thornfield Hall and very little has changed. According to Charlotte Lamb, a very successful Mills & Boon author (100 novels in 20 years), who appeared on the February 1993 BBC2 programme already mentioned, this is what is required. The men must be over-whelmingly attractive and successful in business; they must be experienced, but as another author, Kay Thorpe, pointed out, in these days of AIDS they must not be promiscuous and should take precautions. This was very occasionally done in the novels I read; far more frequently the couple were so busy drowning in each other's eyes, melting and burning etc, that they had no time to think about AIDS. However condoms *are* discussed, though, as in the case of Thorpe's *The Alpha Man*, with pregnancy rather than disease as a cause for concern. Alpha Man as it happens *wants* the heroine Zoe to become pregnant, to prove his virility. This is clearly what is expected of European man; especially if he's Greek. In *Passionate Captivity* (1993), Michalis is as usual described as god-like, tall, dark and overwhelmingly handsome; he also treats April in a very primitive way; this novel ends with expressions of dominance and possessiveness that would not have disgraced Othello:

'You expect me to let you have all your own way?'
... 'My life is planned and you are part of it. I want three children and the first will be a boy. Just see that you obey, Miss Stewart.'
... April shivered with delight, melting against him and ready to obey any orders he issued.
'You want an heir,' she said dreamily.
'I want a sign of ownership,' he corrected, his tongue tracing her lips. 'My woman, wearing my rings and carrying my child. You have already given me enough jealousy to last a lifetime. If anyone else ever looks at you! ...' His ardent threat was silenced as his lips crushed hers and he turned her beneath the demanding pressure of his body.[26]

This quotation seems to me to typify all too clearly the essence of the central relationship in all the novels I have read. It also, although it is perhaps more explicit than others, reveals exactly the nature of the hero. He expects his wife to subordinate all to him, her job – April is an interior designer – her home and family in England, and to become his appendage in a country of whose language she knows only one word, *'efharisto'* – 'thankyou'. All the novels I have read offer the dual hero figure, much as Mary Stewart does; the real hero, the one the heroine desperately desires, is of the type outlined above. The other, the false hero, is a much gentler character, less forceful and usually with a weakness of some kind, requiring the heroine's sympathy and even support, but thereby earning also her contempt.

As for the heroine. We look in vain for those positive role models mentioned by Margolies. The only heroine in all the novels I have read who actually organises her own life in the sense of finding a way of making an income, setting up a house and successfully running two businesses, a shop and a farm, is Morna in the historical romance *The Wild Heart* (1986), by Anne Herries. And even here everything she does, including undertaking the hazardous voyage to Australia, is done for the sake of the hero, Jared Trenwith, who of course resents every single thing because he wants to be the master. (He spends much of the interminable narrative either chained up on board ship or as her reluctant bond-slave in the colony, a happy if temporary reversal of the usual slave/master role.)

According to Charlotte Lamb, the heroine should be like the girl next door. According to the discussions overheard during the BBC2 programme, it appears that there are very firm ideas about exactly what she should be like; she should be younger, often ten years younger than the hero, sexually inexperienced, if not actually a virgin, and she should of course be beautiful. All the novels I read, and these are largely 1990s' publications, had heroines who had a job of some kind. Quite often the job, where it takes her, and whom she meets, is central to the story. Many of the heroines also have higher education qualifications, although even if, like Caroline in *Two-Faced Woman* (1991), by Roberta Leigh, she has a degree, the hero has a superior one, in this case a First from Oxford. The jobs they have are often described as high powered; other characters, especially men, especially the hero, reluctantly admire their head for business. But the job is never as important as the man, or the man's job for that matter.

The Mills & Boon editors and authors were anxious to point out that marriage was not the only thing on their heroines' minds, but this is not borne out by the way in which the narratives are told. As with the Harlequins cited above, all the stories are told in the third person, from the point of view of the heroine. Modleski points out that this places the reader in a position superior to the heroine; the reader is not invited to identify totally with the heroine, as she is with the first-person narrative of the

Gothic romance; she, having read other novels, and, occasionally, being allowed a glimpse into the mind of the hero, foreknows
a more positive outcome than the heroine can hope for. Modleski's
further point, related to John Berger's theories in *Ways of Seeing*
(1972), that this objectifies the heroine, reinforces as a fact her
sense of being the object of others' gaze and superior knowledge.

Heroines, despite their jobs, their tastefully furnished flats,
their glamorous clothes, and their often-stated claims to independence, in fact spend a great deal of narrative time worrying
about what other people, especially the hero, think of them,
their looks, their work, their reputations. (Extraordinarily, for
the nineties, the heroine of *Yesterday's Echoes*, is terrified lest her
parents, sister, and the whole town, think that she is having a
'sordid affair' with the hero; the announcement of their
engagement, master-minded by the hero, is not only desirable but
essential.)

What does seem extraordinary is, as Margolies points out,[26] the
degree of insecurity suffered by all these flat-owning, car-owning,
high-powered young women. Unlike the hero who, as well as being
supremely arrogant about them, need never doubt his attractions,
since every woman falls for him and all the men either admire
or resent him, the heroine is never certain of her charms; her beauty
has to be validated over and over again, and especially by the hero.
Ultimately the hollowness of all this apparent equality, of education
and employment, is exposed, because it is indeed hollow for the
heroine whose only real aim, realised by the reader, if not by her,
is the love of the hero. And love is made manifest as far as she is
concerned by his expressions of possession, jealousy of other
men, and by his making love to her. Love making – and Mills &
Boon are anxious to point out that while it is now OK to describe
this, it is never merely sex – is the necessary demonstration of the
true nature of the relationship between hero and heroine. As she
is almost always a virgin, to his surprise and pleasure (since of course
she cannot compare him unfavourably with others), he is the priest
of love, gently initiating her into its mysteries and delights; even
when she has had previous experience, so considerate of her
responses is he that she is overwhelmed by the uniqueness of the
pleasure he gives her. The pleasure she gives him is debatable; often
he will express his gratitude for her generosity, but in fact she is
actually described as the passive recipient of his 'fluttering' kisses,
his 'tenderly stroking', or 'insistently probing' touch, his 'maleness'.
All these descriptions, and there are usually two events to be
described, are recounted in the most delicate way. The words 'penis'

and 'vagina' are never referred to; indeed, probably just because it is possible to talk about them without any problems of possible prurience, breasts and nipples play a dominant part in the encounters. Nipples are sucked and stroked, breasts are cupped and kissed almost to the point of orgasm. Orgasm is never mentioned either, only dark depths, crashing waves, shooting stars et al. But despite all of this eminently satisfying even earth-moving love making, congress alone is not enough. In each plot there is always a literal post-coital tristesse, in that something in the nature of a misunderstanding occurs to separate the lovers and of course make clear to them that what they really want is commitment and marriage.

However marriage can never be attained until the end of the novel; even in *A Rock and a Hard Place* (1992), by Leslie Davis Guccione (a Silhouette text, set in America, on sale in Safeways), where the hero and heroine have been divorced, it takes the whole of the narrative to achieve what is suggested as the only possible outcome – remarriage, not simply reunion. Therefore the plot follows the usual pattern of initial attraction, gradually warming feelings, a night of love, a misunderstanding and estrange-ment, clarification and declaration of undying love, and the usual melting into each other's arms. It is interesting that this novel, under the Desire imprint, is actually more about foreplay than sex; the night of love ends without consummation, when the hero decides to wait.

Heroes deciding to wait is another feature of Mills & Boon novels. One possible interpretation is that they are just too responsible to take advantage of the heroine, who is very often in an upset state – wet, shocked, frightened. Another is that the hero enjoys reducing the heroine to a panting mass of desire just to prove his power over her – sadism again? Another, and this might explain reader pleasure, is that by these endless pseudo-climaxes the plot actually echoes the rhythms of the sex act, as desired, according to letters written to women's magazines, by many women, in which foreplay is infinitely extended and penetration deferred until the last possible moment. This might explain why men find Mills & Boon risible, their chosen 'scripts', as I shall discuss in the Conclusion, being so very different, and why the descriptions of sexual activity are so different from those written by men, especially those written *for* men, in magazines like *Penthouse* and *Forum*.

The plot, as Charlotte Lamb explained, and as the Harlequin tipsheet cited earlier states, must be about love; anything else must be subordinate to that. The problem with this limitation, quite apart from the stultifying effect it must have on writers' creativity, is that as there are only a few ways in which love making can be described the narrative must depend, to a large part, on recounting why the hero and heroine cannot be together. There are two main obstacles in the path of true love: lack of communication, and other women. The repeated failures of heroes and heroines to tell each other what they really feel constitute a large part of most plots. When they do talk to one another, misunderstandings occur and breakdown ensues. Radway argues:

> Romance reading, it would seem, can function as a kind of training for the all-too-common task of reinterpreting a spouse's unsettling actions as the signs of passion, devotion, and love.[28]

This seems to me to be not only optimism of a high order, but radically misguided. In these novels the hero is always in love with the heroine, no matter how he may appear to be feeling. When he does communicate with her it is usually in the kind of language which few real spouses would ever use. A great deal of recent linguistic research into male/female language differences has shown at least one popular theory is actually true; men find it difficult to articulate their feelings in the way women do, and they are less disposed to value conversation as highly.[29] Thus the male language created in these novels is a projection of female desire, rather than a reflection of real-life interaction. If one reads Mills & Boon to learn to read men, one's real-life experiences will be deeply disillusioning. Indeed, in the BBC2 programme the authors agreed that readers liked a lot of dialogue, especially arguments between hero and heroine; this might well be explained by Spender's hypothesis that women usually lose arguments because men criticise the way the women talk, rather than because of the content of their discourse.[30] In a Mills & Boon novel not only does the reader find a wonderfully handsome hero who is a superbly considerate lover, and one who really wants to become committed, but also a man who listens to the heroine and argues with her as an equal – to begin with anyway.

As to the other obstacle in the path of the happy pair, other women, here we find very negative role models. Apart from conventionally caring mothers and mother figures, that is women older than the heroine or long married, the other woman in Mills & Boon usually follows the pattern set in the Gothic romance; she is the opposite of the heroine: a dark opposite. She is usually beautiful, certainly beautiful enough for the heroine to fear the hero may be attracted to her; she is resentful of the heroine and snubs, belittles and undermines her. She may even, as Julia does in *Reluctant Mistress* (1991), by Natalie Fox, actively subvert the heroine's relationship with the hero – a dashing fellow whose exploits fill many a tabloid newspaper's gossip columns – by alerting the tabloid Press to the couple's plight, marooned by floods in his country house, alone together. Other women cannot be relied on for support; Julia's defection is doubly shocking to the heroine since she ensured Julia a job when their previous firm was taken over by the masterful Robert (the hero). Other women, like Alyson in *High Risk*, are bitches, catty and deceitful, lying about their relationship with the hero in order to create a breach between hero and heroine. Women younger than the heroine are usually adoring of her; she is, if not actually then perceived as, a wonderful older sister; the heroine's care of them is similar to that shown by the Gothic heroine to children, and has a similar function: it uses indirect characterisation to demonstrate the loveability of the heroine. The result of this codification of female roles has the effect of rendering the heroine isolated in a threatening world. Mothers are absent or live a long way away; little sisters are too innocent to be involved. (This perception of girls who are often as old as 17 – Gail in *Passionate Captivity*, Sofia in *The Alpha Man* – shows little regard for the actual behaviour and understanding of today's teenagers.) However, what all these tactics achieve is the archetypal situation of the Gothic heroine, orphaned, reliant on herself alone, and with no one to help her to decode the peculiar signals she is receiving from the hero. But while the Gothic heroine, *vide* Mary Stewart *passim*, manifests courage and resourcefulness, the Mills & Boon heroine worries about her hair, her clothes, is unable to eat, retreats into self-absorption: becomes, as Modleski says, the object rather than the subject of the novel.

Does this then empower the reader, as Radway and Modleski suggest? As the reader knows more about the heroine than she does herself, foreknows the inevitable outcome, is she sufficiently distanced from the heroine to be able to learn from her mistakes? Is this even the intention of the writer? To return to Charlotte Lamb's comments: she said that the heroine should be like 'the girl next door'. One of Radway's research sample says:

> Romances hold my interest and do not leave me depressed or up in the air at the end like many modern day books tend to

do. Romances also make me feel good reading them as I identify with the heroine.[31]

Margolies makes much of the fact that the prevailing tone of the novels is uncertainty; the heroine is in fact given all the reasons for insecurity that modern-day equal woman is supposed to have overcome: she worries about her looks, her clothes, what other people think of her, and worst of all whether her job even matters when the hero's needs require her full-time commitment. I find it deeply depressing that the message of *Passionate Captivity* appears to be that in a time of recession you should forget about making a living yourself and find a rich husband to take care of you. If this, written in May 1993, is the message for the millenium then the women's movements have been in vain.

Radway, cited earlier, criticises literary critics for discussing one text in isolation and generalising from it. Modleski and Margolies are more negative than Radway, but shy away from outright rejection. What none of them seems to be prepared to do is to apply to them any of the usual criteria for critically analysing a text. My own limited experience of investigating why women read Mills & Boon has elicited a generally shamefaced response: they pass the time; they're all right to read when you can't sleep; they're short and don't take up too much time. One woman even said she was proud to say she had never read a Mills & Boon novel. Clearly, whatever women get out of them, escape, entertainment, they do not regard them very highly as written texts. This attitude is not found in readers of Daphne du Maurier, Mary Stewart, Dorothy L Sayers, or P D James. So what is it that characterises a Mills & Boon novel as being a kind of subliterary form?

The most obvious criticism is the one I have outlined above: the heroes and heroines are all the same. However, this criticism can be levelled at the Gothic romance too. What makes a Mills & Boon novel less gripping than a Gothic romance is precisely its focus on romance; there is no other plot. Exotic locations are used: Greece in *The Alpha Man*, and *Passionate Captivity*, the Isle of Skye in *Doctor in Skye*, New Zealand in *Pagan Surrender*, present-day Australia in *High Risk*, nineteenth-century Australia in *Wild Heart*. But unlike Mary Stewart, who spends a good deal of time describing her exotic locations and integrating their atmosphere into her novels, so that the plots and character traits are given some credibility, the Mills & Boon writers might just as well be in Surbiton. Their characters inhabit rooms, beautifully furnished rooms, described to the last rug and ornament; they may even wander through gardens; they pass the time in modern offices. But these could all be anywhere; in the end they are merely the backcloth against which the drama of when will she get him unfolds.

Then there is the style. As I said in the Introduction, I am not primarily concerned with discussions of literary style, my argument being more concerned with theme and character, specifically as related to gender roles. However, unlike the style of a Mary Stewart or a P D James, the style of a Mills & Boon novel, rather like the plot structure of a 'blockbuster', does tend to draw the attention of anyone used to reading general popular fiction (Dick Francis, John Le Carre, Joanna Trollope, for example) to its unusualness. One might, if it manifestly had any other purpose than over-simplification, even say it 'foregrounds' itself. Mills & Boon novels are largely written in simple sentences; the semi-colon is virtually unknown. The effect this has on the narrative is to rush it along; sometimes it is as if one is reading a kind of shorthand. This is particularly true of one peculiar device that I have found in only one novel, *Reluctant Mistress*, where the use of adverbs has been abandoned in favour of active, and oddly-coined verbs: '"My turn to apologise," Robert grated against her mouth.'[32] He 'grates' and 'rasps'; she 'tremors' and feels frissons: 'Liza gasped at the onslaught of fevered frisson that tore through her.'[33] They never eat, but 'fork' their food; she doesn't reply frostily, she 'frosts'. This simplification of narrative extends to the central experience too, the 'falling-in-love'. In this novel, as elsewhere, it is not, as in medieval or courtly romance, the sight of the other person that sends the heroine into her tremors and frissons, but touch. The moment they touch, even if proffering a cup of coffee, that's it. Nothing has ever been like this, and the heroine begins her headlong fall into mindless adoration. Often it seems the only reason for giving the heroine a high-powered job is in order to reinforce the effect the hero has on her mind; to say she is unable to think straight is an understatement; she is: 'hopelessly, helplessly in love'.[34] Much of the so-called plot involves the heroine in pretending to herself – and to the hero, of course – that she is not in love with him. The reader is alerted to the true state of affairs by the unaccustomed tears she sheds, by her anger at his advances:

To her shock and horror his mouth swooped down to hers, claimed her lips and held them with force and yet such deep sensuality that her head reeled. When he'd taken his fill he wiped the moisture from her swollen lips with his thumb.

'Don't get any ideas. That's my first and last show of weakness where you are concerned. I was just curious to know what you tasted like. If you did but know it, that glacial reserve of yours is totally transparent. You might have pulled up the drawbridge on your emotions but they are still there.' He tilted her chin once again. 'Soften up, Liza; I wouldn't like to see my advertising director get hurt again.'

He turned and shut the door softly behind him, and for the first time in a very long time Liza Kay allowed a soft tear to trickle down her burning cheeks.[35]

(Not one of the heroines ever thinks of taking these heroic monsters of egotism to court for sexual harassment.)

So it seems fair to say that no one reads a Mills & Boon novel for its literary style or its unique plot structure or its insight into unusual and interesting characters. This might well be the reason why Radway, Margolies and Modleski have concerned themselves not with what the texts are actually like, and it is remarkable that these critics hardly ever actually quote from or analyse the narratives of actual texts, but what the reader may be supposed to get out of them. They have suggested that the woman may rediscover the kind of cherishing care they once had from their mothers (Radway); that the woman may exorcise her just anger against men by identifying with the heroine in her spirited stand against domineering heroes (Modleski); that the woman might find some positive role models in these 'career-women' heroines (Margolies). All of these critics wrote in the early 1980s. Reading Mills & Boon novels of the 1990s I would say that few of these hypotheses are borne out.

The heroes of the May 1993 selection: *High Risk, Pagan Surrender, Yesterday's Echoes,* and above all *Passionate Captivity* are overbearing, dominant and manipulative; they are not in the least interested in the so-called careers of the heroines, and these are just as pathetically vulnerable emotionally, and as physically fragile as any Charlotte M Yonge reader of the 1890s might expect. The stories all repeat the usual pattern; although Carrie in *High Risk* has an illegitimate baby, we are never allowed to see her as active mother, since she is so ill at the outset of the story that the child himself has called in medical help. As I said earlier, and discussed at length in the Introduction, fairytales, with which these are often compared, are actually far more complex and disturbing; they are about the necessary journey we all have to take into the responsibilities and pains of adulthood. Mills & Boon novels can at best be described as escapist; they offer all the challenge of a warm bath or a box of chocolates. At worst they offer a distorted picture of the world in which personal independence matters far less than yielding to a man's desires, and, more perniciously, in which those men are discovered to have concealed beneath their manly chests sensitive and considerate impulses which magically transform their manifest appearance as tyrants into latent carers and lovers. It is not for nothing that Mills & Boon offer the loyal reader a free teddy bear. She'd be safer with that. At least it's real!

5

Deadlier than the Male: Novels by Sally Beauman, Shirley Conran, Jackie Collins

Sade regularly subsumes women to the general class of the weak and therefore the exploited, and so he sees femininity as a mode of experience that transcends gender. Feminine impotence is a quality of the poor, regardless of sex ...

If Justine's image gave birth to several generations of mythically suffering blondes, Juliette's image lies behind the less numinous prospect of a board-room full of glamorous and sexy lady executives ... I see no more resonant image than that of the Cosmopolitan *girl – hard, bright, dazzling, meretricious.*[1]

Carter's 'glamorous and sexy lady executives', playing dominant roles in board and bed rooms, certainly manifest themselves in the bestselling, so-called 'blockbuster' novels of Jackie Collins, Shirley Conran and Sally Beauman. And so, perhaps surprisingly, do the 'mythically suffering', both blonde and brunette. As Sade knew, and Carter points out, Justine and Juliette are simply opposite sides of the same coin, for despite their apparent rootedness in the contemporary world, Collins, Conran, and Beauman all have a great deal in common with Sade's predecessor, Ann Radcliffe, whether in terms of women-as-witch, or plot as event endlessly piled on event. However, the tension between these apparently conflicting presentations of the potential roles of women, between what these writers apparently want to do in their novels and how the novels actually present women, and between the desire to write 'up-to-the-minute', 'in-your-face' novels and the all too familiar baggage of the Gothic, is much more evident here than in the work of writers discussed elsewhere. Throughout her novels Mary Stewart, for example, writes about brave and independent-minded women who struggle on behalf of the forces of good but who find no real problem in sinking back finally, with a happy sigh of relief, into the protective arms of the hero. Collins, Beauman, and especially Conran, seem uncomfortable with their awareness of the changing nature of late twentieth-century woman, and the fact that for her the hero's arms are not enough. Or, rather, what these writers say, is that it *should not* be enough; that a fulfilling job is better than an unequal and dependent role as a mere wife; that women can be as aggressive, as hero-like, as any man.

The ways in which such stories are told, with their 'new' messages for the New Woman naturally differ in style from author to author, but, as I hope to show, they do not differ in substance. All of these authors write the kind of fiction interestingly but debatably described by Avis Lewallen thus:

> Fiction by, about and for women that shows women capable of achieving social, economic and sexual satisfaction is now extremely popular. From a feminist perspective these are contradictory texts: on the one hand, the capitalist ideology that pervades them largely ignores, on a manifest level at least, issues of class, race and gender; but on the other, they problematise and prioritise active sexuality for women in ways that might be regarded as a challenge to the exclusively male gaze of patriarchal structure.[2]

Superficially Lewallen might appear to be correct; *Lace* in particular 'prioritises' the right of women to an active and orgasmic sexuality to the extent of spending a great deal of narrative time describing sexual congress in minute and, it has to be admitted, ultimately repetitive and boring detail. Conran would appear indeed to be challenging patriarchal structures in her evident belief that women have an equal right not only to sexual activity but also to fulfilling sexual activity. Males who finish first are not only not nice but are shown to be unreliable in their everyday lives as well. Thus Robert, Pagan's first husband, who stabs at her with the 'marital chippolata'[3] and fails even to arouse her, let alone fulfil her, is totally under his father's thumb, and in order to 'win' her is forced to that very low tactic the concealment and destruction of Kate's (Pagan's best friend) letters to her and hers to Kate. As Lewallen says:

> Sexual satisfaction is represented as equivalent to a career: a commodity which women have the right to, but which has to be worked for. Orgasm is not shown as a biological function that will merely manifest itself at the right moment but something that is learned and acquired – a kind of social skill – much in the same way as one can learn the proper use of words

like *chauffeur* or *chic*, an essential part of the vocabulary of anyone intending to be successful.[4]

And, as Lewallen further says[5], *Lace* could be regarded as a useful manual on just how to achieve success in this field as in the many others with which the novel, and its sequel, *Lace 2*, concern themselves: how to dress well, how to lose weight and keep slim and fit, how to organise a successful banquet, above all how to decorate a house and particularly a bedroom that is to be the backcloth to all this frenzied seeking after the climactic vaginal orgasm.

A further major theme is the creation of economically successful women, and the problem here is what career to give them. In *Savages* (1987), by Conran, it is made very clear to us, by means of indirect presentation – the comments of the heroine, Isabel's, husband, of other women, and the men with whom she works – that she is too much like a man to be really acceptable in either world. It is perhaps also significant that while the corporate wives are off on their fishing trip, and are therefore spared the violence of the terrorists, Isabel is with the men and, being a woman, is not *just* shot. What happens to her is left to our imagination, but it's nasty enough to spur the other women into escaping into, and surviving with difficulty, the rigours of the jungle.

One favoured solution to the career problem is that found in Mills & Boon novels where *the* occupation for a heroine is interior decoration. The two central women in *Dark Angel* (1990), by Sally Beauman, and one (Maxine) in *Lace*, are interior designers. Kate, in *Lace*, has a very brief and totally unconvincing spell as a Kate Adie kind of journalist, but then becomes the editor of a *Cosmopolitan* type of magazine, for which Judy (another of the *Lace* foursome) does the public relations. Pagan, the least obviously feminine of the foursome, is a charity fundraiser. And Lili, whose search for identity is the apparent main theme of the narrative, is an archetypal victim heroine: a child porn star who becomes a major film actress.

In Collins's *Chances* (1981) there are two heroines: the black and poor Carrie, who naturally has no other resort than to become first a whore and finally the wife, twice, of a rich man; and poor little rich girl, Lucky, the daughter of a quite amazingly unpleasant Italo-American gangster, who 'runs' his businesses for him while he is out of the US evading tax. In fact of course she, like Carrie, is being used by an exploitative man who allows her to front her father's hotel chain while quietly buying it all up and having her lover murdered. None of these women in this respect is ultimately allowed, not just by the men in the novels but by the writers, to get away with challenging patriarchal structures.

There are several ways in which potentially positive female role models are in fact subverted in these novels. One is as indicated above: by giving the heroines careers in areas which men already perceive as proper to women the writers don't fall into the trap of presenting bitch witches who might challenge the male status quo. Secondly these women are always in pursuit of love as well as success. Not just sex. Although Lucky makes much of her rejection of the double moral standard which forbids women the right to the promiscuity of the one-night stand, it is made very clear that she is really only interested in gaining her father's love. Thus the ending of the novel:

> They were inseparable, father and daughter. They renovated the East Hampton house [where Lucky lived as a child until her mother was murdered] and lived there half the year, the rest of the time they spent in Vegas. Lucky in her penthouse suite atop the Magiriano. Gino in his luxurious apartment at the Mirage.
> Often Lucky thought of Marco – and what might have been. Sometimes her thoughts would drift to Steven. [The son of Carrie, and possibly Gino, therefore off-limits.] But she was happy. She had Gino. And together they could own the world.[6]

All the heroines of *Lace* are in pursuit of a man who will fulfil their sexual desires, but more than that they also want a man whom they can respect, and who will be supportive and protective of them. Lewallen makes much[7] of the dominatrice scene in which Judy wins Griffin's grudging respect by tying him up on the bed, cutting his clothes to pieces and using him as a sex object, but this is *one* episode in an extremely long book (926 pages of *Lace: The Complete Story*), in which long and detailed descriptions of women being overcome, melting, carried away on waves of passion, are the norm. Far more representative of male/female relationships is that of Maxine and Charles, one rather reminiscent of *The Story of O*.[8] Although it is Maxine's business sense that has saved Charles, chateau and lifestyle, his insistence that she never wear underwear whenever they are out together, so that he may have her whenever he feels like it, renders her subject to his domination:

Charles was an affectionate and indulgent husband. After a certain amount of initial irritability, he let Maxine take over the organization of their lives and was both proud of and quietly amused by the way she did it. Once in a while he put his foot down, but this happened rarely. Most of the time she had her own way and was allowed to win their occasional arguments, but Charles liked her to remember that this was not because he was doting or henpecked, but simply because he chose to indulge her. He had a special way of reminding his wife of this.

Sometimes on formal occasions Charles would make Maxine gasp or blush or even forget what she meant to say. He could manage this by directing one meaningful look at her. It was a power that he had over her and he enjoyed it immensely, this ability to destroy her calm with that one look that, he knew, made her heart lurch and her groin moisten. Maxine knew exactly what the look meant.[9]

Lewallen also says that Conran treats rape matter-of-factly, that:

the lack of sensationalism attached to it downplays the notions of violation and virginal purity. The characters are not destined to become lifelong victims in any physical, psychological or emotional sense: they have the resources to recover.[10]

This may *appear* to be true for Pagan's response to her rape by Paul, but after her unsuccessful marriage she becomes an alcoholic; Judy spends both novels in search of someone who will truly value her after her rape; and Lili cannot be described as other than an archetypal victim subsequent to her early rape and the fearful abortion without anaesthetic that she undergoes at the age of 13 and which opens *Lace* itself. As for Constance, the Dark Angel of Beauman's novel, there is no doubt that it is her childhood experience of multiple sexual abuse that renders her incapable of sustaining emotional relationships of any kind as an adult. Far from showing us the new free and liberated woman enjoying sex in the casual way the male characters do, as Lewallen's comments seem to imply, these writers emphasise over and over again the sad fact that however successful economically their heroines may be, men regard them merely as sources of sexual pleasure, and, it may be said, in their panting pursuit of the chosen man, and gasping surrender to his embrace, the heroines too indicate their eager willingness for this role. Carrie, in Collins's *Chances*, demonstrates this in a truly depressing way. From the moment she is raped and sold into prostitution by her brother she is no more than 'black pussy', forced to rely on more or less universally exploitative men to protect her from the more physically violent of her clients, save her son from kidnappers *and* give her what little of appreciation she ever finds. Meanwhile Collins's male protagonist, Gino, from a background as deprived and unpromising as Carrie's, is gouging and slashing his way to the top, being a wonderful lover on the side, able to seduce almost any woman he fancies *and* retain their loyalty.

A further obsession shared by all the female protagonists, and one which negates even more clearly their potential as positive female role models is their appearance; more importantly and significantly, how they appear to men. Not only are these women victims of sexual oppression – which in Carrie's and Lili's case is scarcely their fault – they are *fashion* victims. Not for nothing are these novels described by critics as 'shopping' novels. Each item worn by Collins's and Conran's heroines has a designer label. Even in the jungle in *Savages* the life-saving watch is a Swatchwatch. No one simply has a car; it has to be a Porsche, or a Ferrari Mondial. Handbags and luggage are always Gucci, and as for clothes! These possessions construct their identity; when others look at them they will be recognised as women of taste and position. And this brings me to the most important point: these women construct their identity through the reactions of men. They perceive themselves as objects and judge the effectiveness of their construction by the reaction they excite in men. As Tania Modleski says, of the heroines of Harlequin novels,[11] these women bear out what John Berger says in *Ways Of Seeing*:

> She is not naked as she is.
> She is naked as the spectator sees her ...
> To be naked is to be oneself.
> To be nude is to be seen naked by others and yet not recognized for oneself. A naked body has to be seen as an object in order to become a nude. (The sight of it as an object stimulates the use of it as an object.) Nakedness reveals itself. Nudity is placed on display.
> To be naked is to be without disguise.
> To be on display is to have the surface of one's own skin, the hairs of one's own body, turned into a disguise which, in that

situation, can never be discarded. The nude is condemned to never being naked.

> Nudity is a form of dress ...
> She is offering up her femininity as the surveyed.[12]

This point is markedly borne out by the female protagonists of Conran's *Savages*; even when enduring all kinds of hardship and fear, thoughts of how they look occur over and over again not only in the insistent narratorial voice of Conran but in the women's consciousness. One bizarre consequence of this is that as they all become thinner and more agile the ordeal seems to be a necessary and improving experience, rather like a health farm where the penalty for going out of bounds is death rather than mere humiliation. It seems no accident that one of the early passages in the novel details the diet that kept Jackie Kennedy thin:

> All the First Ladies lost weight as soon as they stepped into the White House. Apparently the current chef still had Jacqueline Kennedy's menus. Orange juice, poached egg, bacon and black coffee for her breakfast, total 240 calories; for lunch a cup of consomme, a miniature bowl of salad with French dressing and a grilled hamburger (without the bun), total 250 calories; a cup of tea with a slice of lemon at 5 o'clock left Jackie 500 calories in hand for the evening. She could manage a good meal and a glass of red wine on 500 calories. For instance, artichokes Provencale, leg of lamb marinated with coriander, cucumber salad and peaches in wine. Of course, Jackie only ate a teaspoon of *any* sauce, but look at all the years she'd kept to that diet and how it paid off.[13]

Throughout the *Lace* novels people, women, only ever eat teaspoons of sauce or nothing at all; the number of expensive uneaten lunches that are detailed for the reader's delectation defy belief. And why is this? Because things have changed little since the days of *Gone With The Wind*:

> 'Ef you doan care 'bout how folks talks 'bout dis fambly, Ah does,' she rumbled. 'Ah ain' gwine stand by an' have eve'ybody at de pahty sayin' how you ain' fotched up right. Ah has tole you an' tole you dat you kin allus tell a lady by dat she eat lak a bird. An' Ah ain' aiming ter have you go ter Mist' Wilkes' an'

eat lak a fe'el han' an' gobble lak a hawg ... Young misses whut eats heavy mos' gener'ly doan never ketch husbands.'

'I don't believe it. At that barbecue when you were sick and I didn't eat beforehand, Ashley Wilkes told me he *liked* to see a girl with a healthy appetite.'

Mammy shook her head ominously.

'Whut gempmums says an' whut dey thinks is two diffunt things. An' Ah ain' noticed Mist' Ashley axing fer ter mahy you'.[14]

Oh dear, can it be that what really made Ashley fall in love with Melanie was her birdlike appetite? At least Scarlett was allowed to eat in private; no such luck for Conran's heroines who, like Maxine, think of their figures *all the time*; at the beginning of the story she is starving herself down from a size 16 to a size 12; by its end she has had every possible cosmetic operation to maintain the illusion of slim youthfulness into middle age.

This kind of detail suggests obsession, on the part of the writer as much as her characters, and since references to what they look like when dressed or undressed, in bed or at dinner, recur throughout the course of the narrative, such concerns are likely to suggest to the reader that these matter more than anything else. Certainly the ethics of the exploitation of a Polynesian island by an American mining corporation scarcely merit more than a passing nod in *Savages*. As Lewallen says, in the quotation cited earlier, radicalism in these women's novels rarely targets capitalism *per se*.

How women look matters just as much in Collins's *Chances*. Carrie is concerned with her effect on men; at first her looks are seen as a drawback since they lead to Leroy's prostitution of her, but later they become a means whereby she can manipulate men, or so she thinks. In fact Collins's use of a masculine point of view throughout Carrie's story as well as Gino's renders Carrie an object of male domination rather than mistress of her own destiny. This effect, whether desired or not by Collins, is brought about by her use of male terminology to describe women. The word 'pussy' seems never to be off the page. Collins's much-hyped, and much-mocked outspokenness is in fact simply an annexation of male language and its concomitant expression of male patriarchy. Carrie has a 'juicy slit', 'big tits'; even when she has achieved motherhood and the apparently commanding heights of her own brothel, still Enzio Bonnatti (a hood who is supposed to represent the black to Gino's white) exploits her:

She tried to look interested, but it was difficult sitting naked in a chair like an object. She wanted to scream, get up and run. Enzio Bonnatti never thought of her as a person with feelings. She was just another whore, and he had stables of them all over the city.[15]

Long after she has been reinvented, by another man, not herself, and is richly married, she remembers Enzio with loathing for the way he treated her: 'The sound of his name brought back cruel memories. Bonnatti treating her like a table, a chair, a piece of meat, an inanimate object to play with.'[16] Yet even though she would like to murder him and gets as far as driving to his house armed with a gun, the action is in fact beyond her. Reaction seems the most that she is capable of:

She had 23 dollars left in the world, and another human being growing inside of her. She couldn't just lie in the room she was renting and wait. There were no Prince Charmings in her life who were going to come charging up to Harlem on a white horse ready to rescue her. She had conquered drugs and survived.
Was she going to crumble now?
She was only in her twenties.
She decided to continue living.[17]

(A propos my comments in the previous chapter on Mills & Boon style, Collins too, is in a league of her own; she is enamoured of the simple sentence and where that will not serve for adequate emphasis, capital letters are freely used.)

Presumably Collins has created the character of Lucky to counteract this image of the dominated woman; it is, after all, Lucky who actually shoots Enzio. Collins makes much of the fact that Lucky is as foulmouthed as any man, believing she has a right to a promiscuous lifestyle, bossing her brother and father's partner about, learning about business management. But Lucky's story really comes too late in the narrative to form an effective counterbalance to Carrie. Further, Collins gives so much narrative time to Lucky's father Gino and *his* rise to power that it is his point of view, particularly as far as women and their proper place are concerned, that pervades the novel, reinforcing the image of exploited sex object that emerges From Carrie's story. Here is a sample of Gino's unreconstructed male chauvinism:

God but he loved the feel of pussy.
God but he wished he could find a girl who would say no.[18]

He strode by a hostess named America. Raven hair and long legs. He had honored her once. Not a memorable experience but passable.[19]

'Get out of those goddamn clothes, ' he ordered.' I want you in nothing but stockings, garter belt, and high heels.'
   [Bee, one of Gino's flings] laughed softly, 'I thought you'd never ask.'[20]

Like Clementine earlier in the novel, Bee is desperate for Gino, who casts off women with scant regard for their feelings:

She [Clementine] realized with a sharp feeling in her stomach that she loved him. Love was not peaches and cream. Love was jealousy and possession and gut-wrenching misery.
HE DID NOT WANT HER ANY MORE.[21]

Gino's view of Lucky and her desire to be in the business with him is typical and traditional – she can't:

'Because you're a woman,' Gino replied calmly, 'a married woman who will stay by her husband's side and behave like a proper wife ... And it's about time you had a baby. What are you waiting for anyway?'[22]

Lucky's oft-proclaimed right to personal gratification is clearly intended by Collins to show us a liberated woman:

She wasn't a whore. She wasn't a nymphomaniac. She just liked getting laid occasionally without all the bullshit and hassle of a long relationship. Men had been bedding casual pickups since time began. Why shouldn't women?[23]

In fact the text as opposed to the apparent story tells us something quite other. It is open to question whether this represents a failure of nerve or the triumph of conventional wisdom on Collins's part, but as shown earlier, Lucky, just as much as Carrie, defines herself in relation to men, relies on them to rescue her from disaster and only ever actually does her own dirty work personally once. But when she kills Enzio it is for Gino.

In *Dark Angel* by Sally Beauman, the narrative is for once in the first person, and the narrative voice, apart from the opening page, is female. However, the point of view again seems to be focalised through men. Victoria is a malleable heroine, accepting of what is presented to her as evidence; therefore we see Constance mediated by the reactions she provokes in the male characters in the story. She may ultimately be deemed to be a victim, but a great deal of narrative time is taken to establish her, from pre-puberty, as a manipulative and deceitful mantis, preying on any man unfortunate enough to catch her eye.

The narrative is curiously constructed too, so that we can rarely be sure whose point of view of events is being transmitted through Victoria. For unlike Robert Goddard, whose style of writing and plot structure are somewhat similar to Beauman's, she only rarely allows the reader access to the primary source material which provides the 'evidence' for the story. Thus, we are told that Victoria has access to the journals of Constance, Constance's father, her own mother and father, and the eyewitness testimony of her uncle and his friend. But when she is narrating the story it is never clear just who is constructing the version of reality. This is in itself a much more interesting narrative device than the straightforward flashback of parallel lives that is employed by both Collins and Conran. The suspense over the identity of Edward Shawcross's murderer is maintained far more successfully and effectively than that concerning the maternity and paternity of Lili in *Lace*. However, the blurring of the real truth about Constance and her past relationships with the Cavendish family, and therefore the tension which underlies and ultimately undermines her relationship with the last of the line, Victoria, has the effect of distancing the reader from Constance's real sufferings as a child enduring apparently multiple sexual abuse.

It is perhaps significant that the only sex described in detail in this novel is deviant and often cruel. The spirit of Edward Shawcross and his attitude to women pervades the novel:

All sex, to Shawcross, is dirty: its allure lies in his sense of degradation. In his fastidious mind he associates women with dirt: even when he touches them, even when he pushes his own flesh into their orifices, they disgust him. He loathed them, these soft, giving receptacles, in their sea-weed odours, their wet and sticky effusions. Do they know, Shawcross wonders sometimes, how obscene they look, these women with their fat milky breasts, their ugly wet purses of flesh.[24]

In her relationships with men, his daughter Constance echoes his desire for power, though not his disgust: 'I shall never let him be sure who I am, whether I love him or not. The politics of love, you see. I intend to keep a balance of power.'[25]

If Constance, like Carrie in *Chances*, is a victim, Beauman also offers us alternative images of women. Victoria, despite her successful career (taught her by Constance) as an interior designer, is at once too young, too impressionable, and too naive to confront Constance. No, the intended protagonist is Victoria's mother, Jane. This is expressed overtly in the course of the narrative: 'As women, she and your mother were at opposite extremes. It was a duel of angels.'[26]

Jane, the light as opposed to Constance's dark angel, is not beautiful, but she is rich. She, like Constance, loves Acland, and she, against all the odds, marries him. But she has earned his love, by working as a nurse at the front in France, during World War One. However, as with Collins's Lucky, Jane simply hasn't the narrative time, let alone the reader's sympathy, to the extent that she can actually represent other than a token gesture in the direction of an oppositional reading of potential female role model. Constance, who, by the time she takes over Victoria, is separated from her husband and living in a smart apartment in New York, is a heroine very much in the Conran mould, concerned with dress and décor and designer food. Whatever we learn of her past, it is this Lamia-like aspect of her nature which dominates the presentation of the figure who dominates Victoria's and therefore the reader's consciousness.

All of these writers, as mentioned earlier, seem to be aware, specifically because they often refer overtly to them in their texts, of the two main influences on texts for women written in the late twentieth century: the nineteenth-century heritage of the romance/Gothic/fairytale, and the rise of the women's liberation movement. Beauman appears to reject any message about sisterhood that women's liberation might offer; her women are victims of men; not only Constance, but Maud and Gwen are exploited by the men they have relationships with. But the message of the book seems to be that you cannot trust any woman, especially if she is acting out a maternal role. Constance as Victoria's surrogate mother is deceitful, destructive and possessive; for aid in her predicaments Victoria has to rely on men, whether it be her homosexual uncle's former lover Wexton, quoted above, or the tall, dark and handsome Frank, who meta-morphoses out of the childhood protector Franz-Jacob into what reads like an archetypal Mills & Boon hero figure:

I rested my eyes on his face. Either I had been blind or his face was translated. Where I had judged him brooding, preoccupied and censorious before, I now saw a man whose face conveyed both gentleness and strength. Where I had recited defects, I now recited virtues: intelligence, loyalty, humour and resolve. Was he proud? Yes, but I was glad he was proud. Was he arrogant? Possibly, but I could forgive arrogance, once I saw it as a defence. Was he obstinate? Yes, I thought once or twice, when he glanced up at me, that he looked very obstinate indeed, almost fiercely obstinate – and at that type of obstinacy I rejoiced.[27]

Like her mother, Victoria finds True Love and happiness in marriage; a relationship in which, given Frank's chosen field of research, she will play the submissive role:

Without turning his head or, apparently, breaking his con-centration in any way, he held out his hand to me. I rose and clasped it. His grip tightened. I looked down at his hand. I considered past years, past meetings, past sentences. Goodbye and Hello: the sentences were immaterial.[28]

Victoria's love story too is archetypal; separated by the hands of war and Constance, she and Frank are at first antagonistic to one another, but then dislike becomes regard; their broken engagement serves to strengthen their affection and after enduring the obligatory legendary separation they marry, have children, and live, according to the Afterword, happily ever after. Shades of Jane Eyre. Beauman's sole reference to women's rights appears, as one might expect, in the Jane section of the story:

I'm the Controller, Regimental Base Depot, which is officer ranking, in case you don't know, but they don't give us fancy titles, because the men wouldn't like it.' [Winnie to Jane in Flanders][29]

Beauman counters Constance not with another woman but with Frank, who in true knight errant manner saves Jane from the wreck that Constance would have made of her life:

He was, in a sense, out of tune with the age in which he lived, and would have been even more so during the decade which followed, the 1960s. To Frank, changes in social customs or attitude were meaningless: a moral loner, he had evolved his own code, and his adherence to it was rigorous. I tell you this because it may help you to understand a factor in our relationship which was of central importance – and that was his attitude to Constance. Frank Gerhard had plain beliefs, held passionately. He believed in truthfulness, hard work, marriage, fidelity, children and the importance of family life. Constance, therefore, represented everything which was anathema to him.[30]

Dark Angel is indeed about a dominant woman; one who destroys the lives especially of the men she meets, but in the end she is seen to have lost. It is the values represented by Frank which win. He is the frog prince who awakens the sleeping princess, Victoria, and rescues her from the fortified palace in which she still lives with her wicked god- rather than step- mother, a very late developer at 25.

Pseudo fairytale rather than journey into the self is the underlying structure of *Chances* also. Despite the overt reference to there being no Prince Charming to rescue Carrie from the horrors of pregnancy and poverty in Harlem, quoted above, a Prince Charming *does* save her, albeit much later in the narrative, invents a new past for her, and gives her respectability by marrying her. And despite Lucky's averred intention of being regarded as a surrogate man, she is really what she always was, Daddy's little princess. Rags-to-riches is, as Margaret Marshment says,[31] a theme common to all blockbusters, and it is of course in the nature of fairytales that the riches don't always bring happiness. Nevertheless the stories of Carrie and Gino reinforce the peculiarly American message that anyone can make it, and give to their children, Steven and Lucky respectively, the education and 'chances' they never had.

Conran, of the three writers discussed in this chapter, engages the most overtly with the issues raised by the women's movement. In *Lace* much is made of the four women's sisterhood and solidarity, from their protecting each other at school, through their joint parenthood of Lili, to their support of one another financially and emotionally throughout the various crises they each have to face in their marriages and careers. This support system is overtly praised many times:

Judy hoped that the magazine would give its readers the support that she had found in Kate, Maxine and Pagan. Together, the four of them had certainly brought out the best in each other. Without the other three where would they be? Kate was the only one who had real talent, but she was a quiet mouse who worried too much. Without Judy to push her, she'd probably be an unhappy divorcee, spending too much at Harrods. Without Kate, Pagan would still be a misfit brought up in a privileged world in which she never felt at home – a perplexed, hopeless drunkard. Maxine had gone a long way with her determination and hard work but she would never have been world-famous without Judy to show her to the world, and although Judy was a tough go-getter, she would never have started her own business if Maxine hadn't pushed her into it. Alone, their frailties might have overwhelmed them. Together, they had strength and speed and style – which is what *Verve!* [Judy's and Kate's magazine] was going to push as hard as it could.[32]

What this encomium omits to say is that, apart from Judy, one major thing they all had going for them was money. Even when down and out as the 'hopeless drunkard' referred to above, Pagan still has her own cottage, a private income and a domestic to cook and clean for her. This is, I think, an important omission. These characters may worry about how much money they are making, that is, whether they've got enough rather than whether they ought to have so much, I should hasten to say, but they start from a privileged background. When Kate makes her first disastrous marriage, her father makes her a present of the whole house in London, in which she previously rented a flat. Maxine's father also invests money in her first business venture. These are not ordinary, average women. When Lili encounters poverty it is described in melodramatic terms; her rags-to-riches story is rendered incredible by the absence from it of ordinary people. Was there really no-one at school, or in the neighbourhood to whom she could have turned after her abortion? Her fall into pornography seems contrived to say the least, in order that her beauty shall shine out like a rose from a dunghill. On an earlier page Conran directly attacks the women's liberation movement, for being out of touch with the majority of women:

Kate attended four meetings of the Women's Liberation group, but found them all disappointing. Every woman's experience was considered of utmost importance, however boring. There was much rapping and consciousness-raising, but not much seemed to get *done*. The sisters never seemed to talk about practical considerations; discussion was either directed to experience-sharing or else utopian theorizing. Kate was depressed by the muddled Marxist political thinking ... 'The family is a basic unit of capitalism ... system of oppression ... We must destroy it ... Women are slaves whose function is to service the male workers ... Before the Industrial Revolution the home was the centre of productivity with husband and wife participating equally in work and child-care ...'

Kate started to wonder what could be done for the women who wrote those sacks of letters to her every week. On the whole, they loved their men and depended on them. If they didn't have a man, they wished they did. Kate's consciousness had already been raised by the lawyers after her father's death and before her divorce. She knew society was unfair to women. However, it wasn't about to change overnight. Women would have to tackle injustice slowly, without hate or aggression, which could frighten other women away. Kate wondered what she could do to help the situation. She didn't think there was much point in attending any more meetings.[33]

As Margaret Marshment points out in *The Female Gaze*, writers like Conran are faced with an undoubted problem:

Since it is the logic of liberal feminism, as of liberal anti-racism, that women should be represented 'fairly' throughout the hierarchy – i.e. in proportion to their number in the general population – and should be permitted to prove equality with men in terms of competence and their right to its rewards, the hierarchies themselves are not rejected: merely the dominance of men at the top of them. Socialist feminism has been rightly critical of this position, arguing that, even when the individual is successful (which is, in practice, only possible for a tiny minority), the underlying injustices of the hierarchy as such remain unchallenged; new and greater divisions are created between women based on differences in their wealth and power; and the values of patriarchy, far from being questioned, are further reinforced by women adopting them.

What is less frequently remarked are the pitfalls in the more radical strategy of challenging the hierarchy and its values, at least in respect of representation. The problem here is, first, that if women are never shown occupying conventionally masculine roles, these roles remain exclusively masculine ...

The question is, of course, whether this particular combination [of male and female qualities] can be regarded as a relatively progressive fantasy model for women, or whether it constitutes a co-option of feminist aims and values to a politically regressive message.[34]

Marshment eventually decides in favour of Conran et al, on the grounds that what they offer is preferable to the image of womanhood purveyed by the tabloid press. As fantasy perhaps *Chances* is acceptable; its narrative moves at such a speed and its main protagonists are so far removed from everyday life, especially if you happen to be British, that at no point are you likely to feel you are being given a handbook to success. *Dark Angel* is more of a Gothic romance and therefore operates on a different level; again it deals with times long past, a way of life – that of the landed gentry of the English upper middle class, or the cosmopolitan rich of London and New York between the wars, and, only briefly, with the more recent past. Beauman besides makes no claims for the universality of her dark angel's experience or behaviour. Conran, however, does appear to be doing precisely that. Underlying her novels is something of the proselytising zeal that informed other of her books such as *Superwoman*.

At the end of *Savages* an inordinately long list of acknowledgements is opened by these lines: 'Film producer Malcolm Stuart originally suggested that I write a book about a group of women put under pressure, in strange surroundings, without their menfolk.'[35] If *Lace* was a handbook on how to plan one's wardrobe, menus for every occasion, or the décor of one's house, then *Savages* seems to be a handbook on survival. One result of this is that the novel is mercifully free of those endless descriptions of orgasmic experiences; the lesbian encounter between Patty and Suzy, although described as pleasurable, is never repeated, and in fact serves to drive a wedge between them. This indicates a disappointing feature of the whole adventure; especially if the reader is expecting, in the relative absence of men, some celebration of sisterly cooperation. When the women first escape to the jungle, they are, fortunately for them, and creakingly obviously for the plot, accompanied by the captain of their fishing-boat who proceeds to instruct them in survival techniques. While he is with them, although they are all mature married women, they perceive themselves through his eyes:

All day, the women had worked hard under Jonathan's directions, like a class of students working obediently for their professor. They were still not very friendly with each other, and each was, in her own way, vying for the attention of the only man.[36]

When trying to construct the first raft they quarrel violently:

The fight flared up until all five women were yelling again. Accusations and counter-accusations about bad work on the raft led to more personal attacks. Whereas none of the women could see their own mistakes and weaknesses, for years in Pittsburgh they had all observed each other carefully, so each knew the faults of the others, and like sisters, could deftly aim verbal darts, hitting exactly where it hurt most.[37]

This would confirm men's worst expectations of women and is not necessarily true. It is not in fact true of this group, who are, the narrative tells us, only too aware of their own shortcomings. Conran is not only contradicting herself, but falling into the trap of showing women as competitive bitches, rather than cooperative sisters: women as men see them:

Jonathan thought. Women are all the same – bloody babies when it comes to the test. But give 'em a man – any man – to take the final responsibility, and they'll trot along behind him and do what he tells 'em to do – whatever it is.[38]

Again this is not true; the women here follow Jonathan because he is capable; men would do the same. When Jonathan dies, the group do not coalesce, but split into factions. They quarrel and argue and waste time and energy; this is probably what any group of people might do in their situation, but Conran insists all the time on its being the failure of this particular all-women group.

In fact the actual storyline of *Savages* is tediously reminiscent of the romances Silvana liked reading in her former life:

In romantic fiction, which Silvana loved, the hero is always permanently obsessed by the heroine, whereas in real life, once passion fades, a woman always comes second to a man's career. Silvana never came to terms with the fact that her romantic ideas were unrealistic, so without noticing it she gradually became permanently depressed – a condition that evinced itself as weariness.[39]

Annie has been loved for over 20 years by Harry who despite threats to his job and a general belief that Annie, her husband, and the whole group are dead persists in looking for her, and of course saves her; the hapless Silvana isn't so lucky.

This latent message, that life is like a romance; that the prince will come, underlies the manifest message of all these overtly contemporary and 'liberated' novels. Although in their explicitness and length they appear to be very different from Mills & Boon novels, in fact they purvey the same kind of fantasies. Modleski says that the appeal of soaps is their multitude of narratives and the sense that although some stories may end, others can go on and on.[40] In this too we can see the Radcliffe inheritance; the actual plot is fairly simple, but it is complicated by an interminable series of digressions; events and characters multiply, accreting to the main structure like so many barnacles. The point of this technique is simply to spin out the story as long as possible. No further insights are added as a result of these extras; they are not subplots underlining or deepening the themes of the main plot. Ultimately what they do, of course, is render the narrative ideal for casual reading; the superficiality of the characterisation and the episodic nature of the narrative allow the reader to re-enter the story with ease at any time. This might well explain the appeal of these 'blockbuster' novels; they often have sequels: *Lace* is followed by *Lace 2*; *Chances* is followed by *Lucky*; there seems no reason why *Savages* couldn't have a sequel. But one effect of the multi-story novel, and this particular kind of structural device, the flashback, is an impression of superficiality. It is as if the author were not convinced that she could sustain reader interest in one pair of characters, and must therefore provide us with many. This was not, of course, a problem for writers like Dickens or Tolstoy, but they did not simply offer variations on the same theme. In Conran and Collins the narratives hurtle without depth or introspection over many years; also – and one can even criticise Beauman for this, although her characters have more depth, her story a more complex construction – all of them treat of the extremes only of woman's existence. One must be either rich, in which case one is defined by one's husband/lover, or poor, in which case one must sell one's body on the street. Conran shows that she knows of other kinds of women:

Arthur [Silvana's husband] didn't realise that it was easier to have such magical charm if you were not distracted by life's exasperating realities, such as waiting in the rain for a bus, carrying groceries, arguing with repair men or paying their bills with money you can't afford.[41]

But neither her novels, nor those of Collins and Beauman, offer those women positive role models. Failing the rich prince or the hell of prostitution, perhaps Silvana's fate must be ours: depression and weariness, or the uncertain solace of escape into yet another novel. Only perhaps we'd be better off with a very different kind of novel, as I hope to show in the Conclusion.

Conclusion

She is always the dupe of an experience that she never experiences *as* experience; her innocence invalidates experience and turns it into events, things that happen to her but do not change her. This is the common experience of most women's lives, conducted always in the invisible presence of others who extract the meaning of her experience for themselves and thereby diminish all meaning, so that a seduction, or a birth, or a marriage, the actual events in the lives of most women, the stages of a life, are marginal occurrences in the life of the seducer, the father or the husband.[1]

Understanding the social forces that shape desire is integral to an understanding of sexuality and relationships. Like other social constructions ... sexuality is *scripted*: habitual ways of dealing with sexuality have been institutionalized in family and marital structures and in gender roles. Desire and its expression are embedded in a social context that defines what constitutes a romantic or erotic event. Such institutionalized structures provide a 'blueprint' for behaviors and motives sanctioned by the culture, including why one has sex, with whom, when and where it occurs, and what acts are performed.[2]

My aim in this book has been to investigate and discuss the continuing influence on popular twentieth-century fiction *for* women, *by* women, of those nineteenth-century legacies, the moralistic fairytale, and the melodramatic Gothic tale. With this in mind both of the above quotations seem horribly relevant to the novels I have discussed in this book; self-consciousness, to the point of actual inability to react to or order one's own world, seems to be the all-pervading message of the novels of Anita Brookner and Barbara Pym. And the necessity of adhering to a 'script', imposed by societal expectations and the laying down of strictly defined gender roles and permitted relationships, is the message, latent or overt, of traditional, Gothic, and modern romance novels. Even detective novels, when written by women, conform. Even when appearing to challenge the 'script', the status quo, all the writers I have considered actually reinforce it. This 'script', derived from fairytales, reinforced by the Gothic and romantic novel, and subsequently by nineteenth-century views of what constituted permissible behaviour in women, lays down simple rules. However initially independent or self-sufficient they may appear to be, women are obliged to be passive in the 'adventures' of life. They are permitted to be heroines only if they conform to this expectation; otherwise they are hags or whores and can thus legitimately be hurt or even killed. (There is, as I pointed out in Chapter 2, a deeply sado-masochistic subtext to these novels, hence my quotations from Angela Carter's *The Sadeian Woman* (1979)). These heroines' lives are bound up in waiting; waiting like Snow White in her glass coffin, Sleeping Beauty in her bed, Rapunzel in her tower, for a prince, the hero, to come and kiss them into life and sexual experience. Their subsequent fate is to marry and live happily ever after, although the 'script' is not concerned with this part, the greater, of their lives. As Rose points out (and it should be said here that Rose's argument has to do with the failure of popular fiction to address the needs of gay and lesbian readers, but I feel her evidence actually reveals failure *vis-à-vis* heterosexual readers too), this means that romance is essentially only ever concerned with the courtship phase of a relationship, in other words the least *real* part, the part in which people play games, act roles, are *least* themselves. The lover is unlikely to leave his smelly socks lying about the living room, or do any of the other things a husband may well drive his wife mad by doing, so that she seeks solace in the regaining of that lost pre-lapsarian state, the courtship, in escaping into the popular novel.

A corollary of this 'script' is that life without a man of one's own is unthinkable. Women without a man of their own are pathetic things, old maids, spinsters. Dale Spender was quite right to point out in her *Man Made Language* (1980) that the terms defining the single state have very different resonances depending on whether they apply to men or women. Bachelors are always gay, whatever their age; whilst any woman over 30 without a man is an *old* maid. Maids by this definition, despite being, in romance terms, desirable virgins, and despite their potential for being heroines and the sought-after prizes of heroes, must be young.

Anita Brookner and Barbara Pym may seem, at first glance, with their portrayal of busy groups of women, of unhappy marriages, to be challenging the 'script'. Brookner has indeed said that her *Hotel Du Lac* was a 'Cinderella reversal story'. But by admitting that, Brookner is of course admitting the enduring and undoubtedly seductive power of the 'script'. Stories *ought* to be Cinderella stories. In his review of her most recent novel, *A Family Romance*, Tom Lubbock rightly points out the essence of the Brookner 'script':

> Our heroine and narrator is Jane, born in roughly 1965, but a girl perhaps out of her time; and the book offers a pained but firm apology for the single life she finally determines upon, though conscious that celibacy is not quite the honourable estate it once may have been ...
>
> All the facts are pointed in a single direction. For Jane, and also for the reader, the desperate aunt is the only available model of an outgoing emotional life. Men are impossibly uptight ... or flash bastards ...
>
> Jane's own liaisons ... did not do. For several pages she encounters feminists with 'sharing' relationships, but that flat and rational prospect won't do either ... It is an older voice that speaks with this dire conviction, a bad fairy godmother. But, of course, the Brookner doctrine – the painful destiny of all the virtuous – sounds considerably more impressive if foisted onto a younger one. Miserablist propaganda.[3]

Barbara Pym is perhaps more honest than Brookner in that her busy women, with their jobs and involvement in church life, whether urban or rural, are never in the least doubt about the horrors of the single state. In other words, unlike Brookner's heroines they are never allowed, as Edith is in *Hotel Du Lac*, to *enjoy* their solitude even for a brief time. Life, for Pym's heroines, consists in the pursuit of male company. The heroine of Pym's last novel, *A Few Green Leaves*, in her nurturing behaviour, cooking casseroles for exploitative men, is, despite her educational quali-fications and research interests, just as much a maid, young perhaps rather than old, in search of her curate as Belinda in Pym's earliest published novel, *Some Tame Gazelle*. And despite her often sympathetic and perceptive portrayal of single women of different ages and life experience, Pym, again like Brookner, always seems to see women as at war with one another, always competing, never supportive. No sisterhood for them.

As for Dorothy L Sayers and P D James, they are quite open in their adherence to the 'script'; the mystery can only be properly solved by their hero, using all that sensitivity with which as Rose says, heroes in romantic fiction written for women are always endowed. Apparently heroic women are really only ever allowed to underline the attractiveness and of course intellectual superiority of the hero. Other women fall into the usual pattern of hags, whores and maidens; the latter to be protected or, because this is crime fiction after all, to be the victims; the former to be patronised or worse by the hero.

Janice Radway and Tania Modleski have made much of how women might 'use' romantic texts in order to learn how to 'read' men more successfully. Rose makes a better point: how can this change anything if men do not read these texts? Rose points out that, as with the fairytale, male texts, male 'scripts' are 'Adventure' stories:

> If a woman hopes to have a satisfying and enduring relation-
> ship, how adequate a script does the romance provide? ... it
> encourages women to limit their vision of the world exclusively
> to relationships and look to them to answer all their psycho-
> logical needs ...
>   In the romance script, males are transformed from active,
> aroused and non-emotional characters to ones that are intensely
> passionate, patient and attentive. How familiar are men with
> the script women expect them to fulfill? Are males exposed to
> heroes who become sensitive and ardent bridegrooms at the
> end of the novel? Quite the contrary, most elements of the male
> adventure script are unreconcilable with the romance script ...
>   Beginning with the adventure fairytale, two themes are
> reinforced for male characters: independence and conquest.
> Unlike fairytale heroines who are released from imprisonment
> through heterosexual relationships, heroes are thrust into the
> world unwillingly and have to provide for themselves. The
> plot reassures boys that severing connections with family,
> although terrifying, will lead to success, parental acceptance,
> and female admiration. But adult love relationships are
> ensconsed on the periphery of life.[4]

In this respect Pym and Brookner would seem to be more true to reality; their heroines markedly fail to read men accurately and in Pym's case indeed actually question their roles:

> Men appeared to be so unsubtle, but perhaps it was only by
> contrast with the tortuous delicacy of women, who smothered
> their men under a cloud of sentimental associations – *our* song,
> *our* poem, *our* restaurant – till at last they struggled to break free,

like birds trapped under the heavy black meshes of the strawberry net, she thought, changing her metaphor. Yet she *had* regarded that little restaurant as being hers and Tom's, and it only now occurred to her that it had happened to be near and cheap and that perhaps was all there was to it.[5]

And so they go on to fail in their relationships. Rose suggests that male 'sex-adventure' stories actively promote the view that, for *men*, *women* are unreadable:

The notion that women practically belong to another species is another latent theme of the adventure script. Even in adult oriented science-fiction, spy novels and private-eye type mysteries, women are an unknown quantity.[6]

No notice at all is taken of this situation by romance writers. Even Daphne du Maurier's initially unreadable Max de Winter in *Rebecca* becomes all too easily understandable as he tells us, and his still adoring second wife, that he killed Rebecca because she laughed at him. We are to suppose that the brutal Sir Richard Grenvile in *The King's General* becomes a tender lover when allowed at last to see Honor's wasted limbs. When all the initial obstacles of mistaken identity – as to which of the two attractive males confronting our heroine is actually the hero – have been overcome, Mary Stewart's heroines are only too happy to subside into his arms and, of course, marriage. Mills & Boon writers would, at first sight, appear to be addressing this problem, of communication failure, head on; but this is not in fact the case. The reason why the hero is behaving oddly, not sweeping the heroine at once up in his muscly arms, is *not* because he is, as he might be in life, actually more concerned with his business affairs, even worried about his mortgage but because he is secretly so in love with her that he hardly dares to speak to her let alone touch her. As Modleski says: 'all the while he is being so hateful, he is internally grovelling, grovelling, grovelling.'[7]

As for the novels which supposedly celebrate dominant women, women supposedly in charge of their own destinies, competing with men in their worlds on a level of equality, it seems to me that Jackie Collins, Shirley Conran and Sally Beauman are as deluding as any Mills & Boon writer. As Angela Carter sets out in the quotation cited above, their heroines spend all their time thinking about how they and their actions may appear to others, and especially to men. Their pursuit of the perfect body, the right clothes, the correct décor for their houses reveals this. Their demands for the same rights as men: to swear, to have casual sexual relationships, to be treated equally in affairs of business; these are all surface. Beneath, Lucky and Carrie are lost little girls, seeking the nurturing care they lost with their dead mothers. As Radway points out in 'Women Read the Romance', this 'nurturant' care is exactly what her sample of readers were looking for in the heroes of their favourite romances. It is, as Rose says, not what men are educated to give. Thus the reward of the heroine, the loving arms of the hero, in marriage, is doomed to be a sad awakening indeed, – a life with a silent, confused and confusing partner, a life in which escape into the fantasy world of the romance is eminently desirable. It is no accident that fairytales end, like Jane Austen's novels, with 'and they all lived happily ever after', with no clues at all as to how this state is to be achieved. (Although, to be fair to Austen, she does portray in detail, and with perception, the process of some very unhappy marriages within the frame of the love story which is the apparent focus of the novel).

In her recent study of women's bestsellers in France and the United States, *The Myth Of Superwoman* (1990), Resa L Dudowitz makes the usual claim for the romance: that it should not be criticised as if it were a literary text; that by so doing the critic is in fact criticising the readership rather than the texts. She concludes her book with what seems to me a rather confused piece of special pleading:

> The bestseller is, as John Sutherland (1981) concludes in his study of 1970s bestsellers, not only a potentially powerful instrument for social change which is alas too rarely exploited, it is also an equally important guide for students and critics to understanding contemporary culture. For both these reasons, it is vital for feminist critics of popular women's bestsellers to move away from judging the novels on the existence or absence of progressive messages or insisting, as Michelle Coquillat does in her 1988 study of romantic fiction, that women's popular fiction is a tool used to indoctrinate women to accept their inferior status in society. Rather, the novels must be studied as a response to the cultural hegemony of media practices which continue to depict women as one-dimensional beings – either mother/wife or aggressive businesswoman. By creating a fictional world in which women have stopped apologizing for being both

mother and career woman and in fact insist that it is normal, and a world in which the combination woman/money/power is not threatening, women writers use the novel and popular fiction as a subtle but persistent challenge to a society which too often relegates women to secondary status.[8]

This pious hope is not fulfilled in the novels I have considered for this book. Indeed in the most recent texts, the May 1993 selection of Mills & Boon novels, abandonment of one's career in favour of an old-style retreat to stay-at-home wife and mother is actually advocated.

Dudovitz also undermines the effectiveness of her message by insisting on regarding Margaret Atwood as a writer similar to, and discussed almost in the same breath as, Shirley Conran. I find it very difficult to believe that the readership is the same. Certainly the texts are not. Atwood *does* belong to that group of women writers who have stopped apologising; but she is a difficult and challenging writer, using metaphor and symbolism in a manner quite unknown to the writers I would describe as being popular with a general female readership. She in fact represents one way in which women's fiction can move into the future. But the way of authors published by Virago and The Women's Press is not, I would argue, a popular or populist way. The reasons these presses are *not* attractive to the casual book-buyer, as opposed to the student for example, are not entirely clear. It might be a simple matter of presentation, as I outline later; it might be the ghettoising of these titles at the rear of bookshops, lumping them all together because they are all written by women, regardless of the fact that the writers themselves are very different. The words, 'her tenth bestseller', connote a familiar and therefore attractive reading experience to the reader looking for something to enliven a long journey or entertain her on the beach.

Given the nature of truly popular texts then, in what direction might women's fiction go? As I said in the Introduction, there seem to me to be fairly clear indicators of whither women's fiction can and might go. On the one hand there is no doubting the enduring popularity of the writers I have considered in this book. Following her recent novel, *Stormy Petrel*, all Mary Stewart's earlier novels have been reissued. Following Margaret Forster's very successful and much publicised biography of Daphne du Maurier, many of her novels have been reprinted. Television adaptations have renewed interest in Dorothy L Sayers, P D James and, most recently, Ngaio Marsh. Anita Brookner, Shirley Conran and Jackie

Collins have all recently produced books which have been much reviewed, and even hyped. Conran's latest, *Crimson*, can be purchased together with a free lipstick manufactured by Boots! And Mills & Boon go on and on and on. They may have experimented with other, slightly more explicit imprints, but the bulk of their output remains as discussed in Chapter 4. What other fiction is there that might offer women a different set of models?

The most obviously different way is that of science fiction/fantasy. Once she has escaped from the everyday world and its societal constructs and expectations, the science fiction/fantasy writer can, having created her own world, give women the freedom to act very differently. Women can, to put it at its simplest, become heroes rather than heroines with all the pathetic dependency that term implies. Certainly the warlike Ruric of Mary Gentle's *Golden Witchbreed* (1983) and *Ancient Light* (1987) combines within herself the qualities of passion and combativeness more normally found in heroes. However Ruric is not a woman of this earth, and this is the central problem of science fiction/fantasy. Once we have made the imaginative leap into her world the writer can reconstruct everything: language, societal patterns, gender roles. Can these new ways of being offer anything to women living in this world and this society?

Certainly one could say that the challenge to the accepted pattern is enough, because it opens up other possibilities of behaviour. One might argue further that both Gentle and Marge Piercy in *Woman on the Edge of Time* (1976) offer an interesting perspective on gender and roleplaying, in that they portray the young of their worlds as being genderless; Gentle's 'ashiren' and Piercy's 'pers' do not become sexually mature until they are 14 and can at that point become male or female. No earlier indication of sex attributes is obvious. This suggests a society in which children are brought up in exactly the same way, because there is no such thing as a 'boy' or a 'girl'. Further both Gentle and Piercy show adult males and females as sharing the qualities, both good and bad, of each sex. Piercy even has her men breastfeeding the babies who are bred in a Brooder, thus saving women from being mothers in a purely animal sense. Utopian visions indeed! However the obverse of this is that these worlds are quite separate from our own. Piercy's heroine has to return to the horrors of her real life, abused and incarcerated in a mental home. Sally Miller Gearhart in *The Wanderground* (1979) further removes her women from the depredations of men; they live in sympathetic harmony with nature, in female-only tribes; the only men they will permit near them are asexual or men who have chosen to be feminine. Gearhart's world is said by the blurb on the back cover to: 'provide a Utopian vision of the future that will delight and inspire'.[9] In it men rule the cities and have all the technology but are afraid to come out into the natural world where Gearhart's women commune telepathically with animals and trees, and have achieved telekinesis and the power of flight. Having done all this, it remains unclear how a *modus vivendi* is ever to be achieved between the sexes, and therefore this world looks to have an uncertain future.

However, the real problem of science fiction/fantasy is that it only appeals to a certain segment of the readership. When looking for escape it seems that most women don't wish actually to leave this world, only their version of it. What appears to be much more successful is a version which takes the known and changes it just enough to make it both credible – in terms of setting, clothes, food, hence all those interminable descriptions – and wish fulfilling, in terms of providing those much-desired nurturant heroes whose love can truly transform any reading goosegirl into a princess.

This might explain the popularity of the novels of Joanna Trollope. An article in the *Independent on Sunday* described her arrival on the popular fiction scene thus:

> Until recently, women's bestselling fiction required a heroine who could power her way to the top of a corporation, screwing everyone in her path, all without falling off her Manolo Blahnik high heels. Thousands of pages of pulpy Eighties prose were devoted to the acquisition of couture clothes, private jets and a place in the boardroom. And then the stock market crashed, moderate, revisionist conservatism arrived, and so did Joanna Trollope.[10]

Her novels have, since *The Choir* (1988), become runaway bestsellers, runaway in the sense that perhaps no one quite foresaw their success. However, with two of her novels being serialised for television, she has clearly arrived up there with those other queens of the mini-series, Conran and Collins. Her novels, as Geraldine Bedell notes in the article quoted above, are also on sale in Safeway. So what constitutes their particular appeal? According to Bedell, Trollope sees herself as a modern Jane Austen or Anthony Trollope; her novels certainly evoke a world quite different from the hectic jet-setting, high-fashion world of Conran or Collins or even Mills & Boon. She writes about small communities: Pym-like villages and cathedral closes, where life revolves around seasonal activities, the school term and the church. Her heroines are middle class, married with at least two children, reasonably but not over educated. They have reached a point at which they are dissatisfied with their lives; they are waiting, like all the other princesses, for a new prince to rescue them from their humdrum, although usually financially comfortable, lives. Trollope gives all the mundane details of these lives, the shopping, the school run, the endless dinner parties and fundraising activities. Thus she roots her heroines in territory very recognisable to middle-class readers. Then she supplies the transforming agent. In *The Choir* it is, not surprisingly, a rather dashing and Bohemian music teacher. In *A Village Affair* (1991) it is rather more surprisingly and daringly another woman, equally dashing and Bohemian. What gives later Trollope novels the twist from the usual pattern of the romance novel is that, unlike Sally in *The Choir*, later heroines do not run off with the agent of their transformation. Rather, they realise their self-hood, their ability to survive without a lover, and set up new homes for themselves and of course their children, to whom they are never less than devoted. Money for this enterprise always comes from somewhere, and this is the flaw. What discontented woman, knowing she could move herself, and children, from the family home into another establishment, even one that needed 'doing up', would hesitate? Trollope's novels, for all their persuasive detail of ordinary middle-class life are simply fairytales. The women do not even reject the potential lover; he/she lingers hopefully at the edge of the new life, doubtless to be admitted when the heroine tires of her single state. Trollope, interviewed by Bedell said:

> The trauma of two world wars has given rise to a great deal of questioning, experimental and intellectual fiction. And as a reaction to this arcane, recondite fiction, we had the blockbuster rising as the opposite pole, and really those two have held sway for 25 years. And it isn't writers like me spotting a gap in the market, it's the public instinctively making its wishes felt, because the mood of the Nineties is so different. We're more anxious and sober and realistic than we've been probably since the early 1960s. We've come down to earth with a bump.[11]

But her novels do not reflect this 'bump'; they reflect an image of rural, village England which one associates with Rupert Brooke and 'Miss Read'. The newspaper article says that Trollope has always lived in Gloucestershire; perhaps this explains her always beautiful settings; old churches, village greens, houses elegantly constructed of Cotswold stone. Her heroines too are predictable, always stunningly beautiful, wonderful interior designers, great cooks, resourceful mothers. Positive role models indeed, but just as fabulous as Lucky or Lili. Trollope is perhaps more convincing in her portrayal of men; they are allowed to feel inadequate, to be less than heroic. But if they are then they are discarded. What her heroines want are unusual men; men who have been celibate a long time, as in *The Rector's Wife* (1990), so that their capitulation is a triumph for the heroine; men who have only ever lived for their music as in *The Choir*. Trollope's world is only superficially related to the real world. Despite the introduction of single mothers as heroines in *The Men and the Girls* (1992) and *A Spanish Lover* (1993), despite references in both these novels to unemployment and debt, the problems raised are always solved in a maddeningly simplistic manner. Her stories are just as much escapes into fantasy as any Mills & Boon text.

It has of late become fashionable to talk of the irrelevance of feminism, of the idea that we may now live in a post-feminist era and that there is therefore no further need to write about women's rights. The recent demise of that 1960s beacon of feminism, the magazine *Spare Rib*, would seem to reinforce the truth of this notion. Further, following the rapid rise to prominence of the so-called New Man in the world of advertising, if nowhere else, it has also become fashionable for 'real' men to assert their rights to recognition.

Following the leadership of the writer Robert Bly, men have taken to rediscovering their lost primitive selves by drumming and chanting in woods. It seems it is now *men's* turn to claim *their* rights, women by implication now having the upper hand everywhere. A recent book, by a psychotherapist, Adam Jukes, is entitled *Why Men Hate Women*;[12] in it he explains, if that is the right word, how mothers are to blame for the misogyny of men. His theory is based on the Lacanian notion of the necessary separation of the male child from the mother once he has perceived her as Other. Jukes admits that this separation is initiated by the child, but says men blame their mothers for an apparent rejection and so grow up with a tendency to wreak revenge for this early rejection on other women. Blaming women for men's failings and failures appears also to have become even more fashionable. Ministers on the Tory front bench are currently claiming that the rise in juvenile crime is due to poor parental care, particularly on the part of lone mothers, and that the imminent bankruptcy of the Welfare State is the consequence of young women deliberately becoming pregnant in order to claim state benefits and housing. The fact that the much more probable reason for both of these sad situations, the rise in mass unemployment, especially among young men, is the failure of this and other governments to tackle the decline in heavy industries, is thus conveniently ignored. The blame is displaced on to an easier target, and, for this government in particular, an easy moral target. But, as Sue Slipman has pointed out, the current government aim of forcing single mothers to reveal their child's paternity – so that fathers may be forced back into the family they may have chosen to abandon, or been ejected from because they were abusive and violent – is actually a way of denying women and children all their hard-won twentieth-century rights.[13]

Young women are perhaps all too aware of the true nature of many young men:

> Two young women talking in a park. Their lament takes up a theme of love betrayed which has echoed down the years.
>
> First girl: 'So what happened? I thought you two were getting married.'
>
> Second girl: 'He said he would change but then I heard he had been sleeping with his best friend's girl-friend and then he got into a fight at work and when they sacked him he came back and tried to get his wages out of the till – now everyone's angry with him.'
>
> These young women, no more than 19 years old, have no faith in fairy-tale endings.
>
> Second girl: 'I'm not having him back this time. He's just so selfish.'
>
> First girl: 'So what's new? All men are like that. I wouldn't trust any of them.'
>
> Over the past 20 years, a profound change has taken place in those relationships between men and women that used to form the linchpin of family life. A young woman may start a relationship with high hopes of everlasting love but that often conceals a profound lack of faith in marriage and partnership. Young women are growing up with a new message: don't put your faith in Prince Charming. Learn to drive your own carriage.[14]

Although this scenario is clearly intended to make a point in a forceful and journalistic rather than academic manner, the current climate of opinion would seem to reinforce its underlying truth. And what does current fiction offer such disenchanted young women? More fairytales?

My argument in this book has been concerned with the fact that although feminist critics have been very quick to charge male writers with stereotyping of women, rendering them marginal or subject victims of the heroic and/or predatory male, in truth *women* writers have not done their sex any favours. The reader of the Mills & Boon novel or a modern Gothic would only too easily recognise the heroine of *The Mysteries of Udolpho*, her plight, her reactive passivity, her all too familiar reliance on the hero to save her. Apart from Daphne du Maurier, all the writers I have discussed in this book have been guilty of limiting women's vision of their possible roles, their interpretation of their actual experiences. And this vision of reality is (*pace* Radway et al and the theory of the interactive reader) rendered all too acceptable because the writers discussed avail themselves, quite naturally, of the simple and straightforward narratological devices of the nineteenth-century fairytale and the Gothic novel.

As I said in the Introduction we are all suckers for stories; we become familiar with simple structures from babyhood onwards. We enter into similarly written narratives with patterned expectations, and we are not disappointed. I am not denying the simple pleasures of reading any of the texts I have discussed, nor that all of us, at times, need the comfort of a reliable narrative just as we need the very similar comforts of a hot bath or a box of chocolates. But today's woman, as I queried above, surely needs something more as well?

Certainly a great deal of modern fiction by women *does* offer more. It offers an expansion of the consciousness, an imaginative entry into other kinds of experience. I am aware that this view of the possible function of literature is old-fashioned, even outmoded. Nonetheless I think we have to accept that few people other than literary critics and students actually read texts in the approved Barthesian manner. We are none of us natural deconstructionists either. And, besides, the Shlovsky theory of 'making strange' surely means making the familiar momentarily unfamiliar, so that we may see it for what it really is?

Herein, I think, lies the problem. Too much excellent modern fiction by women is perceived as making too strange the familiar world of the reader. First by means of style; here are two quotations, the first by an acknowledged feminist writing in the genre of the detective story:

> The two women exchanged guilty looks. They had not given the details of the break-in a moment's thought, so keen had they been to avoid the subject in the course of the evening.
>   'Bloody good burglars you'd make,' Geoffrey said scornfully. 'I don't suppose you've brought gloves with you either? ...'
>   Loretta frowned to herself, aware that Geoffrey was taking great pleasure in showing off his superior knowledge.[15]

Joan Smith's Loretta Lawson, despite being a university lecturer and a declared feminist, is ravishingly beautiful; men fall for her throughout the novel(s); and she is always conscious of how she looks to them. And, as here, she often relies on their superior knowledge, strength, old-boy networks, in her detective pursuits. She looks, thinks, and behaves exactly like any of our conventional heroines from Mills & Boon, Mary Stewart or Jackie Collins. No reader would have any difficulty with her style either; as we can see here, it is manifestly transparent. Let us look now at another avowedly feminist writer, Margaret Atwood. This is a quotation from one of her early novels, *Surfacing* (1972):

> He must have been waiting in the village, the searchers must have told him they'd seen me, perhaps he was with them. He stayed behind when David and Anna went away in their car ... what's important is that he's here, a mediator, an ambassador, offering me something: captivity in any of its forms, a new freedom?
>   I watch him, my love for him useless as a third eye or a possibility. If I go with him we will have to talk, wooden houses are obsolete, we can no longer live in spurious peace by avoiding each other, the way it was before, we will have to begin. For us it's necessary, the intercession of words; and we will probably fail, sooner or later, more or less painfully. That's normal, it's the way it happens now and I don't know whether it's worth it or even if I can depend on him, he may have been sent as a trick. But he isn't American, I can see that now; he's only half-formed, and for that reason I can trust him.
>   To trust is to let go. I tense forward, towards the demands and questions, though my feet do not move yet. He calls for me again, balancing on the dock which is neither land nor water,

hands on hips, head thrown back and eyes scanning. His voice is annoyed: he won't wait much longer. But right now he waits.

The lake is quiet, the trees surround me, asking and giving nothing.[16]

These are the closing sentences of the novel and they are scarcely transparent, even to someone who has read the whole novel. The present tense alone is disorienting; when was this written? What is happening here in the mind of the heroine? Who is Joe and what is to become of them both? And what hero is ever described as 'half-formed'? Secondly, ambiguity and opacity distinguish Atwood's narrative; she invites interpretation; she challenges accepted norms both of behaviour (by the kinds of character and situation she writes about) and of plot structure and closure. Like Toni Morrison in *Beloved* (1987), Atwood writes in a kind of prose that is charged with poetic inference, yet at times switches effortlessly into the idioms of everyday speech. Symbolism adds further layers to their stories, so that their texts need to be unpicked, as it were, by the reader. We have to be effortful; we *have* to interact with these narratives in order to make sense of them and what they are telling us of a real world. For although Atwood's novels are rooted in Canada and Morrison's in black America, at no time are we left in doubt that fiction is here being used to illuminate, rather than escape from reality, even when it is agonisingly painful.

Atwood's most recent novel was excerpted in *Cosmopolitan* magazine in November 1993; perhaps this marks her break-out from the ghetto of Virago Press into the popular fiction world of Jilly Cooper and Shirley Conran; I hope so. Although it is laudable of Virago and The Women's Press to have published previously unpublished, out-of-print or underrated women writers – apart from one or two exceptions like *The Color Purple*, they have not met with popular success among the generality of women readers. Even the choice of name, in Virago's case, or the choice of an iron as logo, in the case of The Women's Press seem now perhaps to have been a mistake. Barthes was only too accurate in his comments in *Mythologies* (1973) on the messages conveyed by certain signifiers. Both these publishing houses convey visually an essentially middle-class, intellectual message. Add to that the resultant ghettoising of the books which I referred to earlier, and how then can they compete with Mills & Boon's literal Rose of

Romance, the windswept heroines of the modern Gothic, the mysterious and dramatic covers of the 'blockbuster'?

It is both a positive and a negative that *Beloved* is currently on the 'A' level AEB syllabus; that *The Color Purple* has for some time been a GCSE text. Women need to know that such literature exists; that there are options. However, such prescription may also have a ghettoising effect. The *Cosmopolitan* move seems to me to be the more positive. Interestingly the filming or televising of a novel can suddenly rush it on to the bestseller lists; witness the incredible popularity of *The Color Purple* after Steven Spielberg's film and the interest shown in Edith Wharton subsequent to the success of Martin Scorsese's film of *The Age of Innocence*. Suddenly it seems these writers *are* accessible. What the feminist presses clearly need is more publicity, and perhaps some of the money from those very successful films to aid them in promotion.

For what women need now, perhaps more than ever since the beginning of this century, is the reassurance that they have rights, to individuation, to the realisation of self apart from societal demands and especially male expectation. Now more than ever do they need the support of sisterhood, not of rampant, dungareed, radical feminism, but simply the reassuring support of others who have fought the same battles, and learned that women don't have to play those old seductive roles. They need fiction by writers like Margaret Atwood, who can have her heroine say, at the end of *Cat's Eye*, after a childhood damaged by other women, rather than men:

> This is what I miss, Cordelia: not something that's gone, but something that will never happen. Two old women giggling over their tea ...
> ... Now it's full night, clear, moonless and filled with stars, which are not eternal as was once thought, which are not where we think they are. If they were sounds, they would be echoes, of something that happened millions of years ago: a word made of numbers. Echoes of light, shining out of the midst of nothing.
> It's old light, and there's not much of it. But it's enough to see by.[17]

Women, no less than men, need their *bildungsroman*, which is, as I hope to have indicated, out there, waiting to tell women the truth, not the sad and worn-out fiction; for they need to know that they, like Elaine, can survive the learning experience that is life, and they therefore need fiction that is rooted in the real world. As Wordsworth put it 200 years ago:

Now was it that *both* found, the meek and lofty
Did both find, helpers to their heart's desire,
And stuff at hand, plastic as they could wish, –
Were called upon to exercise their skill,
Not in Utopia, – subterranean fields, –
Or some secreted island, Heaven knows where!
But in the very world, which is the world
Of all of us, – the place where, in the end,
We find our happiness, or not at all![18]

I have a hidden agenda in writing this book; I hope that if teachers read it they will teach both kinds of fiction; if students, that they will read and compare both kinds of fiction. I want all women to experience all the fiction that has been written for them in this century; I want them to experience the comfort and the challenge, the escape and the confrontation, the cooked and the raw.[19] I here use Levi-Strauss's words to describe that essential difference between fiction which confirms our prejudices and simplifies our view of a complex world, and that which, in the popular jargon, 'tells it like it is'. Fiction which presents women as happy victims of dominant and egotistic men does neither sex any favours. We need fiction which paints the world in shades of grey, not black and white, which describes imperfect relationships between imperfect beings and encourages us to make the most of real experiences. We need fiction that does not delude us into making the fatal mistake of the romantic idealist, that of projecting our dreams of an ideal lover on to some hapless, ordinary, but complex and *interesting* real person. For too long we have laid the blame at men's doors; it is women who are their own worst enemies.

Notes

Introduction

1. Sir Philip Sidney, *An Apologie for Poetrie* (1580) p. 52.
2. Jack Zipes, *Fairy Tales and the Art of Subversion* (1983) p. 18.
3. Walter J Ong, *Orality and Literacy: The Technologizing of the Word* (1982).
4. Fanny Burney, *Evelina* (1778) p. 6.
5. Horace Walpole, *The Castle of Otranto* (1764) p. 52.
6. William Beckford, *Vathek* (1782) p. 151.
7. Dale Spender, 'The Semantic Derogation of Women' in *Man Made Language*, second edition (1981) pp. 16–19.
8. The title of a very relevant and lively book, *The Madwoman in the Attic: The Woman Writer and Nineteenth Century Imagination*, by Sandra M Gilbert and Susan Gubar (1979). The term is now used generically in relation to the modern Gothic. It refers of course to the actual presence in Thornfield attic of Bertha Mason, but also to the suggestion that she represents the dark or unacceptable side of female sexuality.
9. Charlotte Brontë, *Jane Eyre* (1847) pp. 140–41.
10. William Wordsworth, *The Prelude* (1805) Book XI, line 142.
11. John Cawelti, 'The Concept of Formula in the Study of Popular Literature', *Journal of Popular Culture* 3, part 3, (1969) p. 385.
12. Sarah Ruth Kozloff, 'Narrative Theory' in *Channels of Discourse*, ed Robert C Allen (1987) p. 55.
13. Janice Radway, 'The Utopian Impulse in Popular Literature: Gothic Romances and "Feminist Protest"', *American Quarterly* (1981) p. 141.
14. John Cawelti, 'Formula in Popular Literature', p. 385.
15. Walter Nash, *Language in Popular Fiction* (1990) p. 24.

Chapter 1

1. Janice Radway, 'The Utopian Impulse in Popular Literature: Gothic Romances and "Feminist Protest"', *American Quarterly* (1981) p. 145.

2. Charlotte Brontë, *Jane Eyre* (1847) pp. 449–50.
3. Daphne du Maurier, *Rebecca* (1938) p. 5.
4. Ibid., p. 283.
5. *Jane Eyre*, pp. 334–45.
6. Ibid., p. 322.
7. *Rebecca*, p. 41.
8. Ibid., p. 57.
9. Ibid., p. 313.
10. Ibid., p. 302.
11. Alison Light, '"Returning To Manderley" – Romance Fiction, Female Sexuality And Class', *Feminist Review* 16, (April 1984) pp. 7–27.
12. *Rebecca*, pp. 355–56.
13. Light, '"Manderley"', p. 12.
14. Ibid., p. 12.
15. *Jane Eyre*, pp. 475–76.
16. *Rebecca*, p. 301.
17. Ibid., p. 298.
18. Cited Judith Cook, *Daphne*, p. 81.
19. Margaret Forster, *Daphne du Maurier* (1993) pp. 251–53.
20. Judith Cook, *Daphne*, p. 182.
21. Daphne du Maurier, *The King's General* (1946) p. 11.
22. *Rebecca*, p. 162.
23. Margaret Forster, *Daphne du Maurier*, p. 214.
24. Judith Cook, *Daphne*, p. 166.
25. Margaret Forster, *Daphne du Maurier*, p. 122.
26. Susan Hill, *Mrs de Winter* (1993).
27. Margaret Forster, *Daphne du Maurier*, for an interesting discussion, *passim*, of what du Maurier called her 'boy-in-a-box', and especially pp. 420–25.
28. Janice Radway, 'Women Read the Romance: The Interaction of Text and Context', *Feminist Studies* 9, vol. 1, (spring 1983) pp. 53–78.
29. Joanna Russ, 'Somebody's Trying to Kill Me and I Think it's my Husband: The Modern Gothic', *Journal of Popular Culture* 6 (spring 1973) pp. 666–89.
30. Mary Stewart, *My Brother Michael* (1959) pp. 226–27.
31. Mary Stewart, *Thunder on the Right* (1957) p. 205.
32. Mary Stewart, *Nine Coaches Waiting* (1958) pp. 140–41.
33. *My Brother Michael*, p. 248.
34. Mary Stewart, *Airs Above the Ground*, p. 228.
35. Mary Stewart, *Madam Will You Talk?*, p. 99.
36. Mary Stewart, *This Rough Magic*, (1964) pp. 165–66.

37. Ibid., p. 214.
38. *Madam Will You Talk?* p. 152.
39. Ibid., pp. 94–5.
40. Mary Stewart, *Touch Not the Cat* (1976) p. 58.
41. Joanna Russ, 'Somebody's Trying to Kill Me and I Think it's my Husband: The Modern Gothic', pp. 687–88.

Chapter 2

1. Tom Lubbock, *Independent on Sunday*, 4 July 1993.
2. Jonathan Coe, *Guardian*, 27 August 1992.
3. Ibid.
4. Anita Brookner, *A Start in Life* (1981) pp. 175–76.
5. Anita Brookner, *Providence* (1982) p. 189.
6. Anita Brookner, *Hotel Du Lac* (1984) pp. 183–84.
7. Anita Brookner, *A Closed Eye* (1991) pp. 254–55.
8. *A Start In Life*, p. 7.
9. *Hotel Du Lac*, p. 27.
10. Ibid., p. 28.
11. Shlomith Rimmon-Kenan, *Narrative Fiction: Contemporary Poetics* (1982).
12. *Hotel Du Lac*, p. 88.
13. Jan Dalley, *Independent on Sunday*, 23 August 1992.
14. John Cawelti, 'The Concept of Formula in the Study of Popular Literature', *Journal of Popular Culture* 3, part 3, (1969) p. 385.
15. *Hotel Du Lac*, p. 28.
16. Ibid., p. 181.
17. Ibid., p. 146.
18. Philip Larkin, cited Hazel Holt, *A Lot to Ask*, p. 251.
19. Janice Rossen, *The World of Barbara Pym* (1987).
20. Barbara Pym, *The Sweet Dove Died* (1978) p. 187.
21. Barbara Pym, *An Unsuitable Attachment* (1982) p. 113. This novel was actually written and rewritten much earlier, and published posthumously.
22. Barbara Pym, Notebook entry, cited Hazel Holt, *A Lot to Ask* (1990) p. 225.
23. Barbara Pym, *Some Tame Gazelle* (1950) p. 5.
24. Barbara Pym, *A Few Green Leaves* (1980) p. 92.
25. Janice Rossen, *The World Of Barbara Pym*, p. 9.
26. This novel was not only written before and during the early years of the war, but arose from a kind of correspondence between Pym and her fellow undergraduates; it was, as I

explain in the text, not published until much later, which might explain why it sounds dated.

27. *Some Tame Gazelle*, p. 119.
28. Janice Rossen, *Barbara Pym*, pp. 151–52.
29. Barbara Pym, Letter To Bob Smith, 8 December, 1963, *A Very Private Eye*, ed Hazel Holt & Hilary Pym (1984) p. 311.
30. Robert Smith, 'How Pleasant To Know Miss Pym', *Ariel: A Review of International English*, vol. 2 (October 1971) pp. 63–8.
31. Barbara Pym, *A Glass of Blessings* (1958) p. 187.
32. *An Unsuitable Attachment*, p. 193.
33. Barbara Pym, *Quartet in Autumn* (1977) p. 65.
34. Ibid., p. 84.
35. Ibid., p. 175.
36. *A Few Green Leaves*, p. 220.
37. *The Sweet Dove Died*, p. 29.
38. Ibid., pp. 158–59.
39. Ibid., p. 170.
40. *An Unsuitable Attachment*, p. 69.
41. Virginia Woolf, *A Room of One's Own* (1929) p. 35.
42. J S Mill, *The Subjection of Women* (1869) p. 242.

Chapter 3

1. Thomas de Quincey, *On Murder Considered as One of the Fine Arts* (1827) cited John Cawelti, *Adventure, Mystery and Romance* (1976), p. 55.
2. Ibid.
3. Ernest Mandel, *Delightful Murder* (1984) p. 16.
4. Dorothy L Sayers, *Gaudy Night* (1935) p. 346.
5. P D James, *Unnatural Causes* (1967) p. 182.
6. Raymond Chandler, cited H R F Keating, *Crime Writers* (1978) p. 53.
7. John Cawelti, *Adventure, Mystery and Romance* (1976) p. 18.
8. P D James, 'Dorothy L Sayers' *Crime Writers*, ed H R F Keating, p. 73.
9. John Cawelti, *Adventure*, p. 18.
10. Ernest Mandel, *Delightful Murder*, p. 2.
11. P D James, *A Taste for Death*, (1986) p. 10.
12. Cited P D James, 'Sayers', p. 71.
13. P D James, 'Sayers', p. 71.
14. Ibid.
15. Ibid.
16. John Cawelti, *Adventure*, p. 106.

17. Dorothy L Sayers, *Introduction to Tales of Detection* (1936), cited P D James, p. 64.
18. *Gaudy Night*, pp. 335–36.
19. R F Ehrlich, cited Dennis Porter, *The Pursuit of Crime: Art and Ideology in Detective Fiction* (1981) p. 155.
20. P D James, 'Sayers', p. 71.
21. Ngaio Marsh, *Death in a White Tie* (1938) pp. 232–33.
22. A feature said by Robin Lakoff, *Language and Women's Place* (1975), to be characteristic of so-called 'women's language'. She does not provide any evidence other than anecdotal.
23. P D James, 'Sayers', p. 71.
24. Dorothy L Sayers, *Gaudy Night*, p. 431.
25. Ibid., p. 282.
26. Dorothy L Sayers, 'Talboys' written 1942, published in a collection of short stories, *Striding Folly* (1972).
27. David Pascoe on an interview with P D James, *Sunday Correspondent*, 1 October 1989.
28. *A Taste For Death*, p. 330.
29. Ibid., p. 382.
30. *Unnatural Causes*, p. 23.
31. *A Taste For Death*, p. 103.
32. P D James, *Devices and Desires*, p. 352.
33. *A Taste for Death*, p. 101.
34. P D James, *An Unsuitable Job for a Woman* (1972) p. 170.
35. Ibid., p. 105.
36. P D James, *The Skull Beneath the Skin* (1982), p. 54.
37. Ibid., p. 264.
38. *A Taste for Death*, p. 228.
39. Ibid., p. 170.
40. Virginia Woolf, *A Room of One's Own* (1929) p. 35.

Chapter 4

1. Ernest Mandel, *Delightful Murder* (1984) p. 26.
2. David Margolies, 'Mills & Boon: Guilt Without Sex', *Red Letters* (winter 1982/3) p. 5.
3. 'Writing Romance Fiction', a half-hour programme shown as part of BBC2, *Night Of Love*, 13 February 1993.
4. Kay Thorpe, *The Alpha Man* (1992) between pp. 96–7.
5. Janice Radway, 'Women Read The Romance: The Interaction Of Text And Context', *Feminist Studies* (1983) p. 54.
6. Tania Modleski, *Loving with a Vengeance: Mass-Produced Fantasies for Women* (1982) p. 45.

7. Ibid.
8. Ibid.
9. Ibid., p. 31.
10. David Margolies, 'Mills & Boon', p. 13.
11. Ibid., p. 6.
12. Tania Modleski, *Loving* p. 32.
13. Ibid., p. 36.
14. Howard M Wolowitz, cited Tania Modleski, *Loving*, p. 57.
15. Janice Radway, 'Women Read', p. 58.
16. David Margolies, 'Mills & Boon', p. 9.
17. Janice Radway, 'Women Read', p. 66.
18. Tania Modleski, *Loving*, p. 58.
19. David Margolies, 'Mills & Boon', pp. 12–13.
20. Susie Orbach, 'The Heart is a Lonely Hunter', *Guardian Weekend*, 13 February 1993.
21. Joanna Russ, 'Somebody's Trying to Kill Me and I Think it's my Husband: The Modern Gothic', *Journal of Popular Culture*, 6, (1973) pp. 666–91.
22. Mary Stewart, *Madam Will You Talk?* (1955), pp. 81–2.
23. Emma Darcy, *High Risk* (1993) pp. 14–15.
24. Robyn Donald, *Pagan Surrender* (1993) p. 16.
25. Margaret O'Neill, *Doctor on Skye* (1992) p. 6.
26. Patricia Wilson, *Passionate Captivity* (1993) p. 189.
27. David Margolies, 'Mills & Boon', p. 11.
28. Janice Radway, 'Women Read', p. 67.
29. Jennifer Coates, *Women, Men and Language* (1986).
30. Dale Spender, *Man Made Language* (1980).
31. Janice Radway, 'Women Read', p. 59.
32. Natalie Fox, *Reluctant Mistress* (1991) p. 112.
33. Ibid., p. 121.
34. *The Alpha Man*, p. 74.
35. *Reluctant Mistress*, p. 25.

Chapter 5

1. Angela Carter, *The Sadeian Woman* (1979) pp. 86–102.
2. Avis Lewallen, 'Lace: Pornography for Women', *The Female Gaze*, eds. Lorraine Gamman and Margaret Marshment (1988) p. 88.
3. Shirley Conran, *Lace: The Complete Story* (1986) p. 284.
4. Avis Lewallen, 'Pornography', p. 90.
5. Ibid., p. 93.
6. Jackie Collins, *Chances* (1981) p. 599.
7. Avis Lewallen, 'Pornography', p. 95.

8. A titillating and even pornographic novel about sado-masochism, told from the point of view of a female narrator. It purports to be by a woman, Pauline Reage, and emerged in mysterious circumstances in France in 1954.

9. *Lace: The Complete Story*, p. 237.

10. Avis Lewallen, 'Pornography', pp. 91–2.

11. Tania Modleski, *Loving with a Vengeance: Mass-Produced Fantasies for Women* (1982), p. 37.

12. John Berger, *Ways of Seeing* (1972), pp. 50–1.

13. Shirley Conran, *Savages* (1987), p. 40.

14. Margaret Mitchell, *Gone with the Wind* (1939) p. 59.

15. *Chances*, p. 331.

16. Ibid., p. 568.

17. Ibid., p. 262.

18. Ibid., p. 13.

19. Ibid., p. 221.

20. Ibid., p. 276.

21. Ibid., p. 222.

22. Ibid., p. 471.

23. Ibid., p. 491.

24. Sally Beauman, *Dark Angel* (1990) pp. 161–62.

25. Ibid., p. 545.

26. Ibid., p. 593.

27. Ibid., p. 725.

28. Ibid., p. 726.

29. Ibid., p. 527.

30. Ibid., p. 750.

31. Margaret Marshment, 'Substantial Women', *The Female Gaze*, p. 31.

32. *Lace: The Complete Story*, p. 499.

33. Ibid., pp. 495–96.

34. Margaret Marshment, 'Substantial Women', p. 33.

35. *Savages*, p. 649.

36. Ibid., p. 272.

37. Ibid., p. 328.

38. Ibid., p. 326.

39. Ibid , pp. 24–25.

40. Tania Modleski, *Loving*, p. 88.

41. *Savages*, p. 30.

Conclusion

1. Angela Carter, *The Sadeian Woman* (1979) p. 51.

2. Suzanna Rose, 'Is Romance Dysfunctional?', *International Journal of Women's Studies*, vol. 8, part 3 (1985) p. 250.

3. Tom Lubbock, *Independent on Sunday*, 4 July 1993.
4. Suzanna Rose, 'Is Romance Dysfunctional?', p. 257.
5. Barbara Pym, *Less than Angels* (1955) pp. 104–5.
6. Suzanna Rose, 'Is Romance Dysfunctional?', p. 259.
7. Tania Modleski, *Loving with a Vengeance* (1982) p. 45.
8. Resa L Dudowitz, *The Myth of Superwoman* (1990) p. 190.
9. Unattributed comment on back cover.
10. Geraldine Bedell, 'Gloucestershire Chronicles', *Independent on Sunday*, 27 June 1993.
11. Ibid.
12. Discussed in Angela Neustatter, 'Boys will be Misogynists', *Independent*, 7 July 1993.
13. Quoted in Mary Braid and Helen Nowicka, 'Sharp Division on Solution to the Crisis of Family Life', *Independent*, 8 July 1993.
14. Angela Phillips, 'Prince Charming? Haven't Seen Him for Ages', *Independent*, 8 July 1993.
15. Joan Smith, *A Masculine Ending* (1987) p. 67.
16. Margaret Atwood, *Surfacing* (1972) p. 186.
17. Margaret Atwood, *Cat's Eye* (1988) p. 421.
18. William Wordsworth, *The Prelude*, Book XI (1805) lines 136–44.
19. Claude Levi-Strauss, *The Raw and the Cooked* (1962).

Bibliography

The second publication date following some texts indicates texts referred to in the body of this book.

Primary Texts

Atwood, Margaret (1972) *Surfacing* (London: Virago Press).

—— (1988) *Cat's Eye* (London: Virago Press).

Austen, Jane (1818) *Northanger Abbey* (1962, London: Everyman).

Beauman, Sally (1990) *Dark Angel* (London: Bantam Books).

Beckford, William (1782) *Vathek* in *Three Gothic Novels* (1968, Harmondsworth: Penguin).

Brontë, Charlotte (1847) *Jane Eyre* (1985, Harmondsworth: Penguin).

—— (1853) *Villette* (1985, Harmondsworth: Penguin).

Brontë, Emily (1847) *Wuthering Heights* (1987, Harmondsworth: Penguin).

Brookner, Anita (1982) *A Start in Life* (London: Triad Grafton).

—— (1982) *Providence* (London: Triad Grafton).

—— (1984) *Hotel Du Lac* (London: Triad/Panther).

—— (1986) *A Misalliance* (London: Grafton).

—— (1989) *Lewis Percy* (Harmondsworth: Penguin).

—— (1991) *A Closed Eye* (Harmondsworth: Penguin).

Burney, Fanny (1778) *Evelina* (1962, London: Everyman).

Carter, Angela ed (1990) *The Virago Book of Fairy Tales I* (London: Virago Press).

Collins, Jackie (1981) *Chances* (London: Pan Books).

Conran, Shirley (1986) *Lace: The Complete Story* (Harmondsworth: Penguin).

—— (1987) *Savages* (London: Pan Books).

du Maurier, Daphne (1936) *Jamaica Inn* (1964, Harmondsworth: Penguin).

—— (1938) *Rebecca* (1975, Harmondsworth: Penguin).

—— (1941) *Frenchman's Creek* (1965, Harmondsworth: Penguin).

—— (1946) *The King's General* (1969, Harmondsworth: Penguin).

—— (1951) *My Cousin Rachel* (1966, Harmondsworth: Penguin).

—— (1957) *The Scapegoat* (Harmondsworth: Penguin).

—— (1969) *The House on the Strand* Harmondsworth: Penguin).

—— (1971) 'Don't Look Now', *Not After Midnight* (London: Gollancz).

Gearhart, Sally (1979) *The Wanderground* (London: The Women's Press).

Gentle, Mary (1983) *Golden Witchbreed* (London: Arrow Books).

—— (1987) *Ancient Light* (London: Victor Gollancz).

Hill, Susan (1993) *Mrs de Winter* (London: Sinclair Stevenson).

James, P D (1962) *Cover her Face* (London: Sphere Books).

—— (1967) *Unnatural Causes* (London: Sphere Books).

—— (1972) *An Unsuitable Job for a Woman* (London: Sphere Books).

—— (1975) *The Black Tower* (London: Sphere Books).

—— (1982) *The Skull Beneath the Skin* (London: Sphere Books).

—— (1986) *A Taste for Death* (Harmondsworth: Penguin).

—— (1989) *Devices and Desires* (London: Faber & Faber).

—— (1992) *The Children of Men* (London: Faber & Faber).

Marsh, Ngaio (1938) *Artists in Crime* (London: Fontana Books).

—— (1938) *Death in a White Tie* (London: Fontana Books).

—— (1968) *A Clutch of Constables* (London: Fontana Books).

Mitchell, Margaret (1939) *Gone with the Wind* (London: Macmillan).

Morrison, Toni (1987) *Beloved* (London: Picador).

Olsen, Tilly (1962) *Tell Me a Riddle* (1980, London: Virago Press).

—— (1973) *Yonnondio* (1980, London: Virago Press).

Piercy, Marge (1976) *Woman on the Edge of Time* (London: The Women's Press).

Pym, Barbara (1950) *Some Tame Gazelle* (1986, London: Grafton Books).

—— (1955) *Less Than Angels* (1993, London: Pan Books.

—— (1958) *A Glass of Blessings* (1980, Harmondsworth: Penguin).

—— (1961) *No Fond Return of Love* (London: Grafton Books).

—— (1977) *Quartet in Autumn* (London: Grafton Books).

—— (1978) *The Sweet Dove Died* (London: Grafton Books).

—— (1980) *A Few Green Leaves* (London: Grafton Books).

—— (1988) *An Unsuitable Attachment* (London: Grafton Books, posthumous publication).

Radcliffe, Ann (1794) *The Mysteries of Udolpho* (1968: London: Everyman).

Reage, Pauline (1954) *The Story of O* (London: Olympia Press).

Sayers, Dorothy L (1930) *Strong Poison* (1987, London: Hodder & Stoughton).

—— (1931) *Five Red Herrings* (1986, London: Hodder & Stoughton).

—— (1932) *Have his Carcase* (1987, London: Hodder & Stoughton).

—— (1933) *Murder Must Advertise* (1986, London: Hodder & Stoughton).

—— (1934) *The Nine Tailors* (1986, London: Hodder & Stoughton).

—— (1935) *Gaudy Night* (1987, London: Hodder & Stoughton).

—— (1936) *Busman's Honeymoon* (1988, London: Hodder & Stoughton).

—— (1972) 'Talboys', *Striding Folly* (London: New English Library).

Smith, Joan (1987) *A Masculine Ending* (London: Faber & Faber.

Stewart, Mary (1955) *Madam Will You Talk?* (London: Hodder & Stoughton).

—— (1957) *Thunder on The Right* (London: Hodder & Stoughton).

—— (1958) *Nine Coaches Waiting* (London: Hodder & Stoughton).

—— (1959) *My Brother Michael* (London: Hodder & Stoughton).

—— (1962) *The Moonspinners* (London: Hodder & Stoughton).

—— (1964) *This Rough Magic* (London: Hodder & Stoughton.

—— (1965) *Airs Above the Ground* (London: Hodder & Stoughton).

—— (1967) *The Gabriel Hounds* (London: Hodder & Stoughton).

—— (1976) *Touch not the Cat* (London: Coronet Books).

—— (1988) *Thornyhold* (London: Coronet Books).

—— (1991) *Stormy Petrel* (London: Coronet Books).

Trollope, Joanna, (1988) *The Choir* (London: Black Swan).

—— (1991) *A Village Affair* (London: Black Swan).

—— (1991) *The Rector's Wife* (London: Black Swan).

—— (1992) *The Men and the Girls* (London: Black Swan).

—— (1993) *A Spanish Lover* (London: Black Swan).

Walker, Alice (1983) *The Color Purple* (London: The Women's Press).

Walpole, Horace (1764) *The Castle of Otranto* in *Three Gothic Novels* (1968, Harmondsworth: Penguin).

Woolf, Virginia (1929) *A Room of One's Own* (1985, London: Grafton Books).

Wordsworth, William (1969) *Poetical Works* eds Hutchinson, T. and de Selincourt, E. (London: Oxford University Press).

Silhouette and Mills & Boon Texts

Darcy, Emma (1993) *High Risk* (Richmond: Mills & Boon).

Donald Robyn (1993) *Pagan Surrender* (Richmond: Mills & Boon).

Fox, Natalie (1991) *Reluctant Mistress* (Richmond: Mills & Boon).

George, Catherine (1991) *Leader of the Pack* (Richmond: Mills & Boon).

Guccione, Leslie Davis (1992) *A Rock and a Hard Place* (London: Silhouette Books).
Herries, Anne (1986) *The Wild Heart* (Richmond: Mills & Boon).
Jordan, Penny (1993) *Yesterday's Echoes* (Richmond: Mills & Boon).
Leigh, Roberta (1991) *Two-faced Woman* (Richmond: Mills & Boon).
O'Neill, Margaret (1992) *Doctor on Skye* (Richmond: Mills & Boon).
Thorpe, Kay (1992) *The Alpha Man* (Richmond: Mills & Boon).
Wilson, Patricia (1993) *Passionate Captivity* (Richmond: Mills & Boon).

Critical Texts

Allen, R C ed (1987) *Channels of Discourse* (UK: Methuen).
Armitt, Lucie ed (1991) *Where No Man Has Gone Before: Women and Science Fiction* (London: Routledge).
Atwood, Margaret (1976) 'The Surfacing of Women's Spiritual Quest', *Signs-Chicago*, winter, pp. 329–30.
Baehr, Helen and Dyer, Gillian eds (1987) *Boxed In: Women and Television* (London: Pandora).
Barthes, Roland (1973) *Mythologies* (London: Paladin).
BBC2 *Bookmark, Miss Pym's Day Out* (6 January 1993).
—— *Night of Love: A Guide to Writing Romantic Fiction* (13 February 1993).
Bedell, Geraldine (1993) 'Gloucestershire Chronicles' *Independent on Sunday* (27 June 1993).
Berger, John (1972) *Ways of Seeing* (London: BBC).
Bettelheim, Bruno (1976) *The Uses of Enchantment: The Meaning and Importance of Fairy Tales* (New York: Knopf).
Betterton, Rosemary ed (1987) *Looking on: Images of Femininity in the Visual Arts and Media* (London: Pandora Press).
Binyon, T J (1989) *Murder Will Out, The Detective in Fiction* (Oxford: Oxford University Press).
Bloom, Clive ed (1990) *Twentieth-Century Suspense, the Thriller Comes of Age* (London: Macmillan).
Braid, Mary and Nowicka, Helen (1993) 'Sharp Division on Solution to the Crisis of Family Life', *Independent* (8 July 1993).
Cameron, Deborah and Fraser, Elizabeth (1986) *Lust to Kill* (London: Methuen).
Carr, Helen ed (1989) *From My Guy to Sci-Fi* (London: Pandora Press).
Carter, Angela (1979) *The Sadeian Woman* (London: Virago Press).
Cawelti, John (1969) 'The Concept of Formula in Popular Culture', *Journal of Popular Culture*, 3, Part 3, pp. 381–90.

—— (1976) *Adventure, Mystery and Romance: Formula Stories as Art and Popular Culture* (Chicago: University Of Chicago Press).

Coates, Jennifer (1986) *Women, Men and Language*, (London: Longman).

Coe, Jonathan (1992) 'An Abuse Of Good Behaviour', *Guardian* (August 27 1992).

Cook, Judith (1991) *Daphne: A Portrait of Daphne du Maurier* (London: Corgi Books).

Cornillon, Susan Koppelman ed (1972) *Images of Women in Fiction* (USA: Bowling Green University Press).

Dalley, Jan (1992) 'Sympathy For The Bedevilled', *Independent on Sunday* (23 August 1992).

Dudowitz, Resa L (1990) *The Myth of Superwoman: Women's Bestsellers in France and the United States* (London: Routledge).

Dyer, Gillian (1982) *Advertising as Communication* (London: Methuen).

Eagleton, Mary ed (1986) *Feminist Literary Theory: A Reader* (Oxford: Basil Blackwell).

Ellmann, Mary (1968) *Thinking About Women* (London: Virago Press).

Forster, Margaret (1993) *Daphne du Maurier* (London: Chatto & Windus).

Gamman, Lorraine and Marshment, Margaret eds (1988) *The Female Gaze: Women as Viewers of Popular Culture* (London: The Women's Press).

Graham, Robert (1984) 'Cumbered with Much Serving: Barbara Pym's "Excellent Women"', *Mosaic* 1984, Part 17, pp. 141–60.

Gilbert, Sandra M and Gubar, Susan (1979) *The Madwoman in the Attic: The Woman Writer and the Nineteenth Century Imagination* (New Haven, Conn: Yale University Press).

Holt, Hazel and Pym, Hilary eds (1985) *A Very Private Eye: The Diaries, Letters and Notebooks of Barbara Pym* (GB: Sphere Books).

Holt, Hazel (1990) *A Lot to Ask: A Life of Barbara Pym* (GB: Sphere Books).

Jones, Elizabeth et al (1983) 'Creating Fiction for Women', *Communication Research* 10, Part 1, pp. 111–37.

Keating, H R F ed (1978) *Crime Writers* (London: BBC).

Lambert, Angela (1993) 'Shirley's Message from Monaco', *Independent*, 8 June 1993.

Lakoff, Robin (1975) *Language and Women's Place* (New York: Harper Colophon Books).

Levi-Strauss, Claude (1962) *The Raw and the Cooked* (New York: Harper & Row).

Light, Alison (1984) '"Returning To Manderley" – Romance Fiction, Female Sexuality And Class', *Feminist Review* 16, April, pp. 7–27.

Mandel, Ernest (1984) *Delightful Murder* (London: Pluto Press).

Margolies, David (1982/3) 'Mills & Boon: Guilt Without Sex', *Red Letters* 14, winter, pp. 5–13.

Marxist-Feminist Literature Collective, The (1978) 'Women's Writing: Jane Eyre, Shirley, Villette, Aurora Leigh', *Ideology and Consciousness* 3, pp. 27–48.

Mill, J S (1869) *The Subjection of Women* (1977, London: Everyman).

Modleski, Tania (1984) *Loving with a Vengeance: Mass-Produced Fantasies for Women* (London: Routledge).

Nash, Walter (1990) *Language in Popular Fiction* (London: Routledge).

Neustatter, Angela (1993) 'Boys will be Misogynists', *Independent*, 7 July 1993.

Ong, Walter J (1982) *Orality and Literacy: The Technologizing of the Word* (London: Methuen).

Orbach, Susie (1993) 'The Heart is a Lonely Hunter', *Guardian Weekend*, 13 February 1993.

Pascoe, David (1989) 'Nothing is Safe when Life is an Incurable Disease', *Sunday Correspondent*, 1 October 1989.

Phillips, Angela (1993) 'Prince Charming? Haven't Seen Him for Ages', *Independent*, 9 July 1993.

Porter, Denis (1981) *The Pursuit of Crime: Art and Ideology in Detective Fiction* (New Haven and London: Yale University Press).

Radford, Jean ed (1986) *The Progress of Romance: The Politics of Popular Fiction* (London: Routledge & Kegan Paul.

Radway, Janice A (1981) 'Utopian Impulse in Popular Literature: Gothic Romances and "Feminist Protest"', *American Quarterly* 33, summer, pp. 140–62.

—— (1983) 'Women Read the Romance: The Interaction of Text and Context', *Feminist Studies* 9, 1, spring, pp. 53–78.

—— (1984) *Reading the Romance: Women, Patriarchy, and Popular Literature* (Chapel Hill: University Of North Carolina Press).

Rimmon-Kenan, Shlomith (1983) *Narrative Fiction: Contemporary Poetics* (London: Methuen).

Rose, Suzanna (1985) 'Is Romance Dysfunctional?' *International Journal of Women's Studies* 8, 3, pp. 250–65.

Rossen, Janice (1987) *The World of Barbara Pym* (London: Macmillan).

Russ, Joanna (1973) 'Somebody's Trying to Kill Me and I Think it's my Husband: The Modern Gothic', *Journal of Popular Culture* 6, spring, pp. 666–89.

Showalter, Elaine (1989) *Speaking of Gender* (London: Routledge).

Sidney, Sir Philip (1580) *An Apologie for Poetrie* (1961, Oxford: Oxford University Press).

Smith, Joan (1989) *Misogynies* (London: Faber & Faber).

Smith, Robert (1971) 'How Pleasant to Know Miss Pym', *Ariel: A Review of International English*, vol. 2, October, pp. 63–8.

Spender, Dale (1980) *Man Made Language* (London: Routledge & Kegan Paul).

Sutherland, John (1981) *Bestsellers: Popular Fiction of the 1970s* (London: Routledge & Kegan Paul).

Snitow, Ann Barr (1979) 'Mass Market Romance: Pornography for Women is Different', *Feminist Literary Theory: A Reader*, ed Eagleton, Mary.

Thurston, Carol M (1987) *The Romance Revolution: Erotic Novels for Women and the Quest for a New Identity* (Urbana: University Of Illinois).

Todd, Janet (1980) *Gender and Literary Voice* (USA: Holmes & Meier).

Tolkien, J R R (1964) *Tree and Leaf* (London: George Allen & Unwin).

Zipes, Jack (1983) *Fairytales and the Art of Subversion* (New York: Wildman Press).

Index

Published by Pluto Press

It's My Party

Reading Twentieth Century Women's Writing

Edited by Gina Wisker

The variety and vitality of women's writing in the twentieth century has inspired a fascinating study of popular fiction written by women who, in many cases, were skirting the mainstream. The essays collected here focus on women in popular fictional modes (for example science fiction and detective fiction) and women whose work has been widely read (including Jean Rhys, Agatha Christie and Winifred Holtby).

It's My Party is divided into two parts, the first concentrating on sexuality and representation and on context and deconstruction, the second on gender and genre: a critical celebration of women's reappropriation of hitherto male defined popular fictional genres. Themes explored include magazine fiction and serialised television and cinema adaptations.

ISBN hardback: 0 7453 0679 9 softback: 0 7453 0680 2

Order from your local bookseller or contact the publisher on 0181 348 2724.

Pluto Press
345 Archway Road, London N6 5AA
5500 Central Avenue, Boulder, Colorado 80301, USA

Published by Pluto Press

Changing Our Lives
Women In/to Women's Studies

GABRIELE GRIFFIN

☐   *Ideal for anyone entering Women's Studies courses.*

Women's Studies is now an established course subject in many universities and colleges. This history of the development of Women's Studies offers both lay readers and those specialising in the subject a unique overview of the discipline.

Gabriele Griffin covers the establishment of Women's Studies as a discipline; its relation to feminism and to liberation movements; a discussion of its institutional status; its contents and methodologies with special emphasis on the personal—political dimension and an outline of the issues raised by students on Women's Studies courses.

A feature of the book is a series of interviews providing an integrated personal narrative of the interviewees' experiences of Women's Studies.

Gabriele Griffin teaches English and Women's Studies at Nene College, Northampton.

ISBNs hardback: 0 7453 0752 3   softback: 0 7453 0753 1

Order from your local bookseller or contact the publisher on
0181 348 2724.

Pluto Press 345 Archway Road, London N6 5AA